Straight Line Crazy

David Hare's first full-length play was produced in 1970. Since then he has written over thirty stage plays and thirty screenplays for film and television. The plays include *Plenty*, *Pravda* (with Howard Brenton), *The Secret Rapture*, *Racing Demon*, *Skylight*, *Amy's View*, *The Blue Room*, *Via Dolorosa*, *Stuff Happens*, *The Absence of War*, *The Judas Kiss*, *The Red Barn*, *The Moderate Soprano* and *Beat the Devil*. For cinema, he has written *The Hours*, *The Reader*, *Damage*, *Denial*, *Wetherby* and *The White Crow*, among others, while his television films include *Licking Hitler*, the *Worricker Trilogy*, *Collateral* and *Roadkill*. In a millennial poll of the greatest plays of the twentieth century, five of the top hundred were his.

DAVID HARE

Straight Line Crazy

faber

First published in 2022
by Faber and Faber Limited
74–77 Great Russell Street, London WC1B 3DA

Typeset by Brighton Gray
Printed and bound in the UK by CPI Group (Ltd), Croydon CR0 4YY

A CIP record for this book
is available from the British Library

ISBN 978–0–571–363049

For Nicole, my love

Straight Line Crazy premiered at the Bridge Theatre, London, on 23 March 2022. The cast was as follows:

Robert Moses Ralph Fiennes
Jane Jacobs Helen Schlesinger
Henry Vanderbilt Guy Paul
Stamford Fergus David Bromley
Finnuala Connell Siobhán Cullen
Ariel Porter Samuel Barnett
Governor Al Smith Danny Webb
Mariah Heller Alisha Bailey
Shirley Hayes Alana Maria
Sandy McQuade Al Coppola
Lewis Mason Ian Kirkby
Carol Amis Dani Moseley
Nicole Savage Mary Stillwaggon Stewart

All other parts played by members of the company

Director Nicholas Hytner
Designer Bob Crowley
Lighting Designer Jessica Hung Han Yun
Sound Designer George Dennis
Composer George Fenton

Characters

Robert Moses
Jane Jacobs
Henry Vanderbilt
Stamford Fergus
Finnuala Connell
Ariel Porter
Governor Al Smith
Mariah Heller

Shirley Hayes
Sandy McQuade
Lewis Mason
Carol Amis
Nicole Savage

Setting

New York State, 1926–1955

STRAIGHT LINE CRAZY

'The American people never carry an umbrella.
They prepare to walk in eternal sunshine.'

Al Smith

Note

Some of the characters in this play – including Robert Moses, Jane Jacobs, Al Smith and Shirley Hayes – lived and breathed. The actions and biographies I attribute to them are broadly accurate, and sourced from the many books, articles and films which address the transformation of New York State in the mid-twentieth century. Some of the other characters are invented.

Moses' life is so prodigious and his reach so great that I have chosen to concentrate on just two decisive moments in his extraordinary career.

Act One

ONE

Music, deep, romantic. Robert Moses appears on the southern Long Island shore, the sand below, the rollers and sky behind. He's thirty-eight, powerful, imposing, dressed in a frayed shirt and old corduroys, as if his clothes never came off.

Moses It doesn't take long to reach the depths. It doesn't take long to reach the silence. And from there you can look back at the land. You can study the coast.

It's an error to believe that swimming is a matter of strength. It isn't. It's a matter of rhythm. It's not clever to splash around, to spend a huge amount of effort and not move.

I see people do that. I'm not impressed.

The further I swim the happier I am. At night, best of all. So how do I feel when people say 'We were worried. You were gone so long. We called the coastguard.' How do I feel? I tell them 'Why did you panic? Nothing's going to happen to me.'

TWO

The music swells and the image changes. At the other side stands Jane Jacobs. She's an apparently unassuming woman in her forties, sandalled, straight grey hair, wearing a shapeless sack dress. She's surrounded by banners reading 'SAVE WASHINGTON SQUARE'.

Jacobs Human beings don't leave very much behind. When we're gone, what will be left of us? By my reckoning, two things only. Cities and songs. Almost everything that's any good is what nobody saw coming.

I don't mind the villains. Villains are villains. They hate spontaneity and they hate life. They know who they are.

The people I despise are the victims. I'd rather be anything than a victim. If you're educated, if you're able-bodied, if you're born to decent folk, and you live in a warm house, it's wrong to be a victim.

I'll go further. It's wicked to be a victim. That's what I think.

THREE

At once, with the speed of a film cut, Stamford Fergus, sixties, a butler, is approaching Henry Vanderbilt, an assured tycoon, reading in an armchair. Both are archaically dressed. The surroundings are palatial. It's 1926.

Fergus Sir, I'm sorry to tell you this, but there's somebody at the door.

Vanderbilt At the door?

Fergus Yes, sir.

Vanderbilt What do you mean at the door? You mean at the door of our house?

Fergus Yes, sir.

Vanderbilt How is that possible?

Fergus Sorry, sir, but he walked up the drive.

Vanderbilt Uninvited?

Fergus lets the question hang.

And the gentleman's name?

Fergus His name is Mr Moses.

Vanderbilt A visit from the Old Testament. How bracing. Show him in.

Fergus goes, and returns with Moses, holding his hat in his hands. His boots are wet, and sand is clinging to them. Vanderbilt stands.

Moses Robert Moses.

Vanderbilt My friends say that you're an impossible man to meet, and yet here you are.

Moses Then I don't need to introduce myself.

Vanderbilt Fergus has announced you.

Moses Thank you, Fergus.

Vanderbilt Your reputation precedes you.

Moses I thought I had no reputation. I'm in public service. I'm not out to make a name for myself.

Vanderbilt Then you've failed already. Do you need refreshment?

Moses Not urgently.

Vanderbilt Then we can release Fergus. Thank you.

Fergus Sir.

Fergus goes.

Vanderbilt They tell me you're a Yale man.

Moses Yes, sir, I am. Class of '09. I was admitted early.

Vanderbilt Why was that?

Moses My examination results were outstanding.

Vanderbilt Unfortunately, a Yale education is no longer a guarantee of anything.

Moses I believe you're a Yale man yourself.

Vanderbilt You make my point for me.

Moses smiles politely at Vanderbilt's joke.

Moses It's not the only thing we have in common.

Vanderbilt Namely?

Moses A shared love of the exceptional quiet and beauty of Long Island.

Vanderbilt You will need to prove that if I am to be convinced.

Moses I swim down on the South Shore on a beach five miles long.

Vanderbilt I know that. You've been seen.

Moses The best swimming of my life. 'Come away, O human child, to the waters and the wild.' That stretch of beach brings Yeats to mind every time I visit.

Vanderbilt looks at him mistrustfully.

Vanderbilt And when you swim, are you troubled by other swimmers?

Moses Never.

Vanderbilt Then there you are.

Moses I have a five-mile sand spit all to myself.

Vanderbilt And do you play golf?

Moses I do not, sir.

Vanderbilt I'm not surprised. Timber Point has just one hundred members. When I tee off on a Saturday morning, perhaps I see one or two other players, amid the red deer and the pheasant.

Moses It must be enjoyable.

Vanderbilt My point: Long Island depends for its exceptional quiet and beauty on its isolation. Seek to share that beauty and the beauty is gone.

Moses I would agree with you, sir, but.

Vanderbilt But what?

Moses shrugs.

Moses You must face the facts.

Vanderbilt I don't expect such a common cliché from a Yale man.

Moses Nevertheless. Where are we? Not so many miles from what was once a small trading post. A hundred and fifty years on, the city of New York is the capital of the world. Its population has grown by seven million in little over a hundred years.

Vanderbilt So?

Moses Your friend Henry Ford has instituted the practice of giving his employees an annual holiday.

Vanderbilt I warned him against it.

Moses The working week has been reduced from seventy hours to a mere forty-five.

Vanderbilt That's also Henry's doing.

Moses Mr Vanderbilt, the people have discovered a new occupation. It's called leisure. And one day it will be as popular as work.

Vanderbilt I hope not.

Moses The people will spill out of city in the suffocating summer heat, just as water spills from an overfilled jug. They will discover this little paradise which is Nassau County. Is it better they come here like indigents, trampling down the dunes and throwing off their clothes all over the strand? Littering and polluting? Or is it better we build facilities, well-thought-out, well-organised, clean, inspiring?

Vanderbilt Why do they have to come here at all?

Moses Why did you come here?

Vanderbilt It's hardly the same question.

Moses Isn't it?

Vanderbilt No.

Moses Why not?

Vanderbilt Because the Vanderbilts bought property here.

Moses Ah.

Vanderbilt It's ours. It belongs to us. Our family has owned it for many years.

Moses I am told a hundred.

Vanderbilt And if you trouble yourself to read the Constitution –

Moses I know long passages by heart –

Vanderbilt You will find the right to own property is sacred. Landowners have rights which other citizens do not enjoy.

Moses shrugs slightly.

Moses I have no problem with that. Access is what we're talking about, not ownership. Access, Mr Vanderbilt. You know what our Governor Al Smith has said? 'Between the few and the many, I cast my lot with the many.'

Vanderbilt You talk like a revolutionary.

Moses To the contrary. The very opposite. My aim is to forestall revolution, not to incite it.

Vanderbilt How?

Moses The people will get to the beach, one way or another. Let's work together to prevent them doing so by violence.

Vanderbilt shakes his head.

This is a new age. People are waking up and looking around. They want to swim and play tennis, and lay out baseball diamonds, and – yes – even play golf. They want exercise.

Vanderbilt If that's what they want, let them have it. There's plenty of space. All they have to do is make for the setting sun. The American injunction is 'Go West'. Going East is un-American.

Moses It's only for a season.

Vanderbilt looks hard at him.

Vanderbilt Moses, you crawl into my living room like Vladimir Lenin, your clothes tatterdemalion, clutching your hat in your hand and spouting Irish doggerel. Bringing with you, it seems, a good part of Jones Beach.

He nods at Moses' shoes. Moses lifts a heel to look.

Moses I apologise.

Vanderbilt And you dare to tell me we must bow to the mob.

Moses I have not said that.

Vanderbilt I was not sent the memorandum which said that the people are now in charge.

Moses Surely you don't doubt that people have rights?

Vanderbilt Certain rights.

Moses Good.

Vanderbilt But no rights which overrule the rights of property.

Moses Another thing Al Smith taught me: the cure for the evils of democracy is more democracy.

Vanderbilt If you believe that, then you're stupider than you look.

Moses That's always possible.

Moses, charming, smiles at his own concession.

Vanderbilt You say the people will spill out of the city.

Moses Assuredly.

Vanderbilt With their picnic baskets and their songs and their filthy children.

Moses Indeed.

Vanderbilt Why do they have to come here?

Moses Jones Beach is a mere twenty-five miles from Times Square. Why are they not free to enjoy it?

Vanderbilt Because they have Coney Island. They have Brighton Beach.

Moses These places are open sewers, as well you know, presided over by lox and bagel merchants. Awash with tawdry advertisements and so-called amusements, which amuse no one. If there's one thing I despise, it's a boardwalk.

Vanderbilt And now Jones Beach, you say, is to be a sewer too –

Moses Not at all. I'm planning something much more elevating –

Vanderbilt Why do you arrive at something perfect and immediately set out to defile it?

Moses Its beauty will remain unspoiled, I promise. But only if you consent to my arrangements.

Now it is Moses who is digging in.

I am proposing two highways.

Vanderbilt I have heard.

Moses The Southern State Parkway and the Northern State Parkway.

Vanderbilt Is that what you call them?

Moses New roads, free of traffic lights. Sculpted among gorgeous woods and parks.

Vanderbilt *Across* gorgeous woods and parks, Mr Moses. Not among.

Moses The great scandal of Long Island has always been the desperate state of its roads, kept, clearly, in deliberate disrepair.

Vanderbilt Deliberate?

Moses Of course.

Vanderbilt What proof do you have?

Moses It's a strategy by landowners to frustrate travel.

Vanderbilt Are you accusing us of running them down?

Moses I am.

Vanderbilt With what evidence?

Moses Every summer those few adventurous souls who dare to head this way are brought to a halt, as their overheated engines expire on badly maintained tracks. Everything possible is done to discourage them. Well, no longer. My new parkways will make travelling as attractive as arriving.

Vanderbilt shakes his head.

Vanderbilt We have already met to discuss these roads.

Moses Who has met?

Vanderbilt The interested parties.

Moses Was this a public meeting?

Vanderbilt Don't be ridiculous. You would know the names of the families who were there.

Moses I can guess at them.

Vanderbilt Go ahead.

Vanderbilt waits a moment.

No, really.

Moses I would hazard the Morgans.

Vanderbilt Certainly. The J. P. Morgans were present.

Moses The Harknesses?

Vanderbilt Yes.

Moses The Fricks?

Vanderbilt Yes.

Moses The Winthrops?

Vanderbilt Yes.

Moses The Whitneys? The Mackays? The Phipps? The Spreckels?

Vanderbilt You are correct. You are dangerously well informed.

Moses In fact, all the great landowning families of the North Shore.

Vanderbilt Oh, not just the North, sir. The South Shore also.

Moses And what was decided at the meeting?

Vanderbilt What you must expect.

Moses Which is?

Vanderbilt Impassioned and intransigent opposition to all your plans.

Moses I see.

Vanderbilt Unified, organised, and unyielding. At the meeting, your methods of seizing land were compared to those of Napoleon.

Moses Crikey.

Moses smiles, as though his business were done.

Thank you.

He turns to go.

Vanderbilt Are you leaving?

Moses Yes. Why not?

Vanderbilt We've scarcely begun to talk.

Moses So?

Vanderbilt I had imagined we would engage.

Moses I came here to listen. I've listened.

Vanderbilt You're done?

Moses It's part of the planning process. Henceforth when I'm asked 'Did you meet with the critics of the scheme?' I will be able to say 'I met with them.' We call it consultation.

Vanderbilt You've been here hardly ten minutes.

Moses Do I need more?

Moses makes for the door, but Vanderbilt calls out in some irritation.

Vanderbilt Are you not able to defend your own proposals?

Moses turns, emotion breaking through for the first time.

Moses Able? I am able, yes. Not to brag, but I was president of the Oxford Union.

Vanderbilt Indeed?

Moses I may add, the first American to be so honoured. I excel at debate. The question is not whether I am able, it's whether I am willing, given that the door is shut against me.

Vanderbilt Try.

Moses pauses a moment.

Moses Very well. You seek to tell me what it is to be an American. But may I remind you of the other principle of Americanism?

Vanderbilt And what is that?

Moses How has our country managed to advance so fast? How have we overtaken every other economy in the world?

Vanderbilt Tell me.

Moses The dynamo of capitalism is restlessness. Nothing is ever enough. For us, nothing is ever settled. We are always on the move.

Vanderbilt I agree.

Moses You know Yosemite? You know Yellowstone? Those are national parks, and very fine they are too. But I have a new idea. I'll create state parks – huge swathes of untamed countryside, crossed with trails where you can hike all day, fill your lungs and go on down to the water. How do you think it's going to look?

He points towards New York City.

How will it appear – to the broiling masses out there – if I go back to the city and say that the plans I have for a beachside paradise, a place of vigour and health and relaxation, are being stymied at the will of a few old men?

Vanderbilt Is that how you would describe us?

Moses Is it not accurate?

Moses stops, smiling.

Remember, sir, you made your millions out of the despised kikes and wops, living in the tenements you own. Now you wish me to go back and tell the workers that you intend to deny them a day out in the country.

Vanderbilt In our part of the country.

Moses If you continue to shut them out, you may find you have a fight on your hands.

Vanderbilt We welcome the fight.

Moses Good. I too am ready for it.

Vanderbilt Once the landowners of Long Island realise that they cannot go to bed at night for fear they wake up to find that their property's been appropriated, then we shall we welcoming anarchy.

Moses No. Democracy.

Vanderbilt Fergus!

With no warning, Vanderbilt has shouted.

Whatever. The matter will be settled by law.

Fergus reappears.

Fergus, Mr Moses is finished here. Leave him at the end of the drive.

FOUR

Finnuala Connell appears before us. She's neat in a simple skirt, hair tied back, orderly, in her mid-twenties.

Finnuala 'He's a hard man to work for. He has high standards.'

That's what someone told me on the first day. And then they added, 'And if you think he's hard on you, let me assure you, he's so much harder on himself.'

They always say that, don't they?

'He's so much harder on himself.'

As if that meant anything at all. Because it's easy, it's easy to be hard on yourself. I am. I should think you are too. Because it's your own choice. But when someone else comes down on you, that's different. Because there is no choice. You either accept it or you step out the way.

FIVE

The dining room at Belmont House. 1926. A wood-panelled Long Island mansion converted into Moses HQ. At its centre, a massive table, loaded with documents and a twenty-foot representation of Long Island, and the proposed route of the two parkways across it. Finnuala turns to find Moses storming in, in his shirtsleeves. Around him are his whip-thin young draughtsmen and -women, all frightened, all harried. His principal assistant is a gentle, dark-haired young man, Ariel Porter, currently under extreme pressure.

Moses This is not what I wanted. This is not what I asked for. The route has been changed.

Porter I promise you, sir, nothing has been changed.

Moses Porter, Porter –

Porter Yes, sir?

Moses Please. Porter. I'm closing my eyes, can you see? I'm closing my eyes.

Moses has closed his eyes.

Do you see?

Porter Yes.

Moses Do you see my eyes closed?

Porter Yes.

Moses Now observe my arm.

Moses moves his arm to delineate a shape in the air.

What is that?

Porter I have no idea.

Moses What shape am I making? With my arm?

Porter is looking for help to the others.

In the air, I am delineating. Tell me what you see.

Porter I just see your arm moving.

Moses I shall move it again.

Moses does so.

Well?

Porter Is it a machine?

Moses No.

Porter Is it some sort of animal?

Moses All right, enough stupidity, Miss Connell will tell us.

Finnuala It's an outline of Long Island.

Moses Correct. Correct! Miss Connell knows. Why don't you?

He opens his eyes and jabs at various points in the air.

Montauk. Stony Brook. Babylon. Amityville. I carry it here. In my head. It's here. In my waking hours and in my sleep. As it should be in yours.

Porter Yes, sir.

Moses How can we call ourselves planners unless we know what we're planning? The artist knows the canvas. The sculptor knows the stone.

He moves closer to Porter, who is terrified.

And the route of the planned Southern State Parkway? As follows: say after me: Hempstead.

Porter Hempstead.

Moses Oyster Bay.

Porter Oyster Bay.

Moses Babylon.

Porter Babylon.

Moses Brookhaven.

Porter Brookhaven.

Moses is jabbing at each point on an imaginary map.

Moses You think you can mislead me?

Porter No.

Moses You think you can deceive me? You traced this map?

Porter Yes.

Moses Personally?

Porter Yes.

Moses You drew it? With your own hand? You copied it from my own projections. And? And?

Moses waits.

Porter I was asked to make one small change.

Moses You were asked? Asked by whom?

Porter As I say –

Moses Not by me!

Porter As I say, when I was tracing, it was put to me that the Whitneys were not happy.

Moses The Whitneys? Unhappy? Who heard of such a thing?

Porter We should not go through their orchard. By taking the natural bend at the southern perimeter of their property,

18

by going with the camber, it was possible to skirt the trees and to preserve the integrity of their estate.

Moses Indeed?

Porter By the smallest possible diversion.

He stares a moment at Moses.

You probably don't know this about me, but I'm a country boy myself.

Moses I didn't know that, no.

Porter Born and raised in Oklahoma.

Moses Really?

Porter I have rural origins.

Moses You have my sympathy.

Porter And my father taught me that it's a crime to kill a tree.

Moses He taught you that?

Porter Be clear, I'm not dogmatic –

Moses Thank God for that –

Porter I'm not doctrinaire.

Moses Well, that's a relief. Because I was myself doctrinaire for many years, and a fat lot of good it did me. Ten years I slaved in the civil service, an idealist, a reformer. And I achieved precisely nothing.

Porter I'm sure that's not true.

Moses It's true.

Porter By all accounts, I've been told your work at the Municipal Civil Service Commission was much admired.

Moses stares hard at him.

Moses Porter, are you pulling my leg?

Porter I wouldn't dare.

Moses Whatever the quality of my work, the Bureau of Standards and the Board of Estimates destroyed it. Entirely and completely.

Porter I'm sorry.

Moses I set out sweeping reforms for the New York civil service. My intention was to restructure local government. Every man would be re-graded and every man would be assessed. Every aspect of his performance would be judged, not annually but monthly. Monthly, Porter. Imagine that.

Porter I'm trying.

Moses Idlers would be rooted out, and backsliders identified.

Porter How wonderful.

Moses There would be real efficiency, evidentially based.

Porter That's marvellous.

Moses And at the end of my labours, what? I left the civil service exactly as I found it. In every detail.

Porter I didn't know that.

Moses A prototype of incompetence and mediocrity.

Porter That bad?

Moses I had wasted my time completely.

Porter I didn't know that either.

Moses There have been many years, Porter, when I might as well not have lived.

Moses nods, more vigorous, more focused.

And shall I tell you the reason? Do you know why I failed?

Porter I don't.

Moses Because I made the mistake of thinking that if I proposed something which was logical, reasonable and effective, people would at once see its merits and fall in behind it.

Porter And they didn't?

Moses They blocked it at every turn.

Porter Why?

Moses Because they always do! That's what they do!

Moses moves away, going over it in his head.

Looking back, I would say my preparations were poor. I was insufficiently thorough. My education had left me ignorant of human psychology, human fear. I was not prepared for their behaviour.

Porter How they behave?

Moses What human beings do. What they do when presented with the unarguable.

Porter What do they do?

Moses They panic. They panic, Porter. I learned some painful lessons in those years. Lessons neither Yale nor Oxford ever taught me.

Porter Lessons about people, you mean?

Moses About un-reason. Un-reason is wired into the human brain.

Porter Really?

Moses So, I tell you, Porter, at the end of all this, if I happen to be planning the optimum route for a highway and I have to chop down a tree, I will chop down a tree.

He laughs, amused at the idea.

Porter Yes, sir.

Moses And if it means that somewhere in the godforsaken state of Oklahoma, your father drops dead in mourning for the living twig, that is a loss I shall bear with fortitude.

He turns and stabs a finger at the map.

Now. Why did you change the direction of the route? Why?

Porter It's barely changed.

Moses I saw the change. I noticed it at once.

Porter It's been changed by a matter of yards.

Moses Give me the reason.

Porter looks down.

Porter The Governor mentioned to me that if we compromised, we would have a better chance of realising our plans.

Moses The Governor said that?

Porter Yes.

Moses You spoke to the Governor?

Porter Yes.

Moses In person? Do you talk to him often?

Porter He came by the office.

Finnuala He came casually.

Moses Thank you, Miss Connell.

Finnuala He dropped by.

Moses This happens a lot?

Porter We're not saying a lot.

Finnuala Once or twice.

Moses And he engages you both in conversation?

Porter looks nervously to Finnuala.

Porter Well, you know how it is, sir. Quite often, you're out walking the shore.

Moses Oh, am I?

Porter You're absent from the office because you also like to take that little boat –

Moses Ah yes –

Porter And examine the shoreline from the perspective of the sea.

Moses You're right. I do like that. I like to see how nature has sculpted the land. It educates me. We're not at war with nature, Porter –

Porter I agree –

Moses We're going with the grain, Porter, not against it.

Finnuala Sometimes your wife calls on the telephone because you're out so late and the dark has come down.

Moses looks at her sharply.

Moses I don't know why you bring Mary into this. Mary is not your concern.

Finnuala Just saying: Mrs Moses calls us here occasionally because she's anxious, sir. She's always very warm and polite.

Moses Mary is an outstanding woman. A woman of outstanding character. She is the rock on which I build my life.

Finnuala I have no doubt of it.

Moses I walk through that door at eight a.m. and who I go home to is my own affair.

Moses is firm. Porter is nervous.

Porter Anyway, as I was saying, occasionally, when you're out, the Governor calls by to see how we're doing –

Moses He appraises the work?

Porter Not 'appraises', no. More, shoots the breeze.

Moses Informally?

Porter And also – not to be indiscreet – he seems specially to enjoy Miss Connell's company –

Moses Is that so?

Porter He enjoys banter with her.

Moses Is that right, Miss Connell?

Finnuala Al Smith is a very charming man.

Moses He is indeed.

Finnuala As my mother would say, charm is his long suit. There are good reasons he's such a popular governor. It's a special gift, I think, to be able to talk naturally to people.

Moses I think so too.

Finnuala To put them at their ease.

Moses He does that, yes.

Finnuala And he does it wonderfully. I think if you run for elected office, you have to have that quality, don't you?

Moses Maybe.

Finnuala You have to make people melt a little. 'I'll do this for Al,' people say, 'because I really like him.'

Moses They say that, do they?

Finnuala Even when it's something which in their heart they don't want to do. He charms them into it. You know the trick of it?

Moses I don't.

Finnuala He treats them as equals. When he's around, everyone's relaxed.

Moses Are they so?

Moses looks at her, thoughtful.

And when he's here, he tears himself away, does he, the Governor, from bantering with Miss Connell to take a look at the plans?

Porter From time to time.

Moses Does he comment on them?

Finnuala Rarely.

Moses And when he does?

Porter He makes some very reasonable points.

Moses In your version, as you had it, he used the word 'compromise'. I'm wondering, did he use that actual word?

Porter 'Compromise'?

Moses Yes.

Porter Well –

Moses Or did you put it in his mouth?

Porter turns, unhappy.

Porter Finnuala, do you recall?

Finnuala His exact wording?

Porter Yes.

Finnuala Ariel, I'm sorry. I don't.

Moses nods, vindicated.

It doesn't matter, does it? What's clear is, the Governor believes there's no point in making enemies when you don't need to.

Moses Does he? Does he, by God?

Finnuala As a general rule. Why offend people when it's not necessary?

Moses Perhaps you don't realise: I called around on the Vanderbilts.

Porter You went to see them? Personally?

Moses Certainly did.

Porter Wow!

Finnuala How was that?

Moses I met the Fricks. I met the J. P. Morgans.

Porter I bet they were pleased to see you.

Moses Oh yes, I've been on a tour of the great families of Long Island. They told me their concerns.

Porter And what were those?

Moses They were concerned that my sandy shoes might spoil their Persian rugs.

They all laugh.

I've seen some beautiful furniture. Chandeliers.

Finnuala I'm sure.

Moses Come along, Porter, if you meet these people, you will know they are intransigent.

Porter That was your conclusion?

Moses It was unmistakeable. They want no roads. They are against new roads on principle.

Porter Yes, but what the Governor's asking is something different.

Moses And what is that?

Porter His point is this: if by taking a road just a few hundred yards out of the way, you can win their trust, why not do it? Make a small concession. What do you lose?

Moses looks at him a moment.

Moses What you lose is your reputation for being strong. What else does an urban planner have?

There is a silence. No one wants to answer.

Once you have a reputation for getting things done, then you can get things done. Simple. Please take away the plans and restore the original route –

Porter Where?

Moses Through the orchard, Porter. Through the orchard of your beloved Whitneys.

Porter looks hesitant.

Take them out of my sight while you do it. All of you. Miss Connell, stay.

The planners all start to leave, taking the plans with them, when Moses suddenly shouts at Porter's departing figure.

Ask yourself, Porter: what have the Whitneys ever done for you?

Moses sits in his favourite hard chair. Finnuala is alone with him.

Moses And I hate even using the words.

Finnuala What words?

Moses 'Urban planner'. The very phrase smacks of weakness.

Finnuala Why?

Moses Plan, plan and never do.

Finnuala Maybe that's how it feels.

There is a moment. Finnuala knows his moods.

Perhaps I could fetch you a root beer.

Moses Root beer doesn't do the job.

Finnuala I can put my hands on a real beer.

Moses Nothing slakes my thirst.

Moses shakes his head.

How long since you joined us?

Finnuala A couple of months.

Moses Yes. It's only two years since I paced the beach, the salt spray in my face, and I had the idea. It came fully formed. Like a vision.

Finnuala All at once?

Moses Like all the best ideas. Faster than shit through a goose.

Finnuala sets to work tidying up the table.

I stood there, taken aback by the beauty, by the isolation, and I thought: this beach could belong to the people.

Finnuala Yes.

Moses To the people!

Finnuala What a wonderful notion.

Moses Thank you, Finnuala. But for the moment, notion is all it is.

Finnuala Come, that's hardly your fault.

Moses Isn't it?

Finnuala You're doing everything you can.

Moses I'm fighting, yes.

Finnuala But the forces of reaction are strong.

Moses looks at her a moment.

Moses You're trained, you say?

Finnuala Yes.

Moses At a school of architecture?

Finnuala Night school.

Moses Where?

Finnuala You wouldn't have heard of it.

Moses You see, I am untrained.

Finnuala I know.

Moses Perhaps that's why planning means nothing to me.

Finnuala You love the planning. Poring over maps. It excites you.

Moses No, you're wrong. I love mixing the concrete, and driving in the stakes.

He shakes his head.

Whenever I have ventured among them, I find planners do nothing but plan.

Finnuala That's their job.

Moses Men who swell with pride at their pretty models, their pretty model buildings and the pretty model people who walk among them. For them, when the plan is made, the job is finished. Because they can go to their conferences and boast. Boast to their friends, boast to their peers. Who cares? It's in the world we have to work.

Finnuala has begun to tidy the table, to put the papers in order. She works methodically. Moses sits in a wooden chair, drumming his fingers.

I'm a ditchdigger, I'm not an academic.

Finnuala Clearly.

Moses I put academia behind me. It's for the young. It's for the inadequate.

She refuses to be provoked.

In ancient Egypt, did anyone plan? I don't think so. After Nero had destroyed Rome by fire, was the rebuilding planned? The great medieval cathedrals, were they planned? No.

Finnuala Things were different then.

Moses Different how?

Finnuala In the obvious ways.

Moses Which are?

Finnuala I hardly need say.

Moses No, tell me.

Finnuala stops, irritated.

Finnuala It's my impression that in Egypt before the birth of our Lord, the views of the people did not need to be considered.

Moses And now they do?

Finnuala So they tell me.

Moses And you think that's right, do you?

Finnuala Certainly, it's right.

Moses We've advanced, have we? We're superior, are we? Superior to the Egyptians?

Finnuala More sensitive perhaps.

Moses Hmm.

Moses thinks about this a moment.

Have you seen the pyramids?

Finnuala I haven't, no.

Moses You should.

Finnuala I would like to.

Moses They're magnificent.

Finnuala So I've been told.

Moses And each pyramid different, each one an advance on the previous.

Finnuala I would love to see them.

Moses They learned as they went along, refining, improving, till the method was perfected.

Finnuala That's enviable.

Moses Everyone in our profession should see the pyramids. They represent a standard of achievement.

Finnuala Unfortunately, buying groceries has been more on my mother's mind than sending me to Cairo. Funny, that.

Moses looks at her, puzzled.

Moses Your family is disadvantaged?

Finnuala Only in money.

Moses What other kind of disadvantage is there?

Finnuala I meant affection.

Moses Oh. Yes.

Finnuala In our house there was no absence of affection.

The other kind seems not to have occurred to him.

Moses Do you not know, there are always ways around financial problems?

Finnuala For you, perhaps.

Moses You think there's that great a difference between us?

Finnuala Of course there's a difference. For goodness' sake.

Moses Because of your circumstances?

Finnuala Oh, please.

She's really annoyed. He waits, inquiring silently.

A walk-up in the Bronx, if you have to know.

Moses Did you say it was just you and your mother?

Finnuala Yes.

Moses Your father?

Finnuala Passed away.

Moses How?

Finnuala Typhus.

Moses You still live with your mother?

Finnuala What do you imagine? An apartment of my own?

She is heavily sarcastic.

Moses So how did you finance your education?

Finnuala I worked as a stenographer.

Moses Admirable.

Finnuala An eighteen-hour day, seven days a week. In the fashion district.

Moses To get you here?

Finnuala Yes.

Moses Working as a draughtsman?

Finnuala Draughtswoman, more accurately.

Moses And you're content? You're content just to plan?

Moses spits out his judgement, vehement.

You see, you're wrong about people and their views.

He's needling her and at last Finnuala rises to it, showing her temper.

Finnuala It seems, according to you, I'm wrong about everything.

Moses Oh?

Finnuala Yes.

Moses Was that a brief display of Irish temperament?

Finnuala No. It was me containing my Irish temperament.

Moses You mean it can get much worse than that?

Finnuala Much.

Moses I would like to see it.

Finnuala Go on as you are and you will.

Moses We saw only a flash. But if the flash is there, for God's sake be grateful, Finnuala, and put it to use. Don't be ashamed.

Finnuala I'm not.

Moses That flash can power change. Temper's as much part of our armoury as intelligence. Temper can build freeways.

Finnuala shakes her head.

Finnuala You're angry with me and I don't know why.

Moses Because you swallow the conventional wisdom.

Finnuala Why should that offend you?

Moses You suck it in like a goombah vacuuming up spaghetti.

Finnuala Can you tell me what in particular I have wrong? If you were not my boss, I would tell you that the high horse is an infuriating place to be addressed from.

Moses is pleased to have so provoked her.

Moses Very well. Your principal error is this: to imagine that the people's views are of any importance at all.

Finnuala I thought you were a democrat.

Moses I am.

Finnuala I thought we were working to improve the people's lives.

Moses We are.

Finnuala Is our aim not to serve them?

Moses It is.

Finnuala So?

Moses We must advance their fortunes without having any respect for their opinions.

Finnuala Is that not a contradiction?

Moses Our job is to lead, not to follow.

Finnuala We also have to stay in touch. We have to know what people want.

Moses I don't agree. People don't know what they want until they have it.

Finnuala How are you so sure?

Moses Because nothing worthwhile has ever been achieved without initial resistance.

Finnuala And is that resistance always wrong-headed?

Moses I believe it is. To build a road, it may be that you need to knock down a house. What happens? A lot of

screaming and shouting. 'That house has always been there.'
And then when the road is built? 'Oh my God, how much
better this is. How did we ever manage without this road?'
They can't even remember the house. The people lack
imagination. The job of the leader is to provide it.

Finnuala What if the leader errs? What if the leader makes
a mistake? Should he not be answerable?

Moses Answerable to whom?

Finnuala Why, to the people.

Moses Heavens, Finnuala. I'm not going to make a
mistake. I've waited so long!

Now it is Moses who is furious. He gets up, impatient.

Ten years! Ten years! Trapped in the interstices of City Hall.
Watching the advancement of my inferiors. Growing more
impatient by the day. They offered me prisons, can you
imagine?

Finnuala No.

Moses 'Do you want to run the prisons?' 'I do not. Why
would I want to lock men up?' 'What do you want then?' 'I
want to set them free. Give me the means to set them free.'

Finnuala What, all of them?

Moses Why not? I despise incarceration. My personality is
not so weak that I need to affirm myself by punishing
others. Flawed I may be, vindictive I am not.

Moses smiles, satisfied.

Finnuala Mr Moses, we know how much the parkways
mean to you. We are keenly aware. All of us.

Moses The roads mean nothing to me. It's the state parks
which have meaning. The roads are just the means of
getting there.

He points a finger at her, aggressive.

And don't think it's one state park, because it isn't.

Finnuala I've begun to realise that.

Moses Oh, it's not enough. One beach? One state park? No. That's what others have done.

Finnuala How many are you planning?

Moses I want to create a model for the rest of America. So that states and counties everywhere take up our example. I'll tell you what it is. It's a *system* of parks. It's a *system* of roads.

Finnuala On what scale exactly?

Moses You'll keep this to yourself?

Finnuala Do you not trust me?

Again, he looks at her, considering her.

Moses Very well. A system of roads and parks all over Long Island. Once the principle is established, there is no end to what we can achieve.

Finnuala Where exactly?

Moses Why not Montauk? Why not Bethpage? Why not Sunken Meadow?

Finnuala But these places are miles apart.

Moses Yes.

Finnuala With different topography.

Moses Not so different.

Finnuala You have all of them in mind?

Moses The land is there. It's waiting.

Finnuala But the practical plans?

Moses shrugs.

Moses Sketched out. Loosely.

Finnuala Where will you get the money?

Moses Tell you something strange, Finnuala. It's much easier to get large sums of money than small.

Finnuala Why is that?

Moses Suggest a shed, nobody's interested. Build a bridge, everyone's in.

Finnuala What's the reason?

Moses Because if a project is large enough, it boggles the mind. And once the mind is boggled, the pockets are open.

Finnuala You think it's that easy?

Moses is fired up, excited.

Moses Finnuala, think about it. Who will stand up and argue against parks? Parks are motherhood and apple pie. Who can be against hiking and fishing and climbing and breathing fresh air? Who doesn't want to crack crabs and drink beer?

Finnuala No one.

Moses Parks are unarguable good. Parks are virtue. By allying myself with virtue, I can achieve anything I want.

He dots the imaginary map in the air again.

One in Caumsett. A perfect spot. Another in Orient Beach. Not bad. And what about that land lying fallow in Hither Hills? Have you thought about it?

Finnuala As far as that?

Moses Why not? Long Island could be the recreation area for the whole of New York City.

Finnuala You see it all joined up?

Moses I do. A pattern of opportunity.

Moses wags a finger, pleased with his next revelation.

And then when Long Island is secured, we move west to the mainland.

Finnuala To the rest of New York State?

Moses Certainly.

Finnuala To do what exactly?

Moses Build more roads. Build more parks.

Finnuala But that's not your purlieu, is it?

Moses Not yet.

Finnuala You run the Long Island State Park Commission.

Moses Thus far.

Finnuala Long Island. That's the limit of your power.

Moses That is an oversight I intend one day to correct.

Finnuala smiles slightly, tickled by the idea.

Finnuala I suppose I have to ask, Mr Moses, is there no end to your ambition?

Moses Why? Should there be?

Moses grins.

I've waited so long. And as of this moment, we have an exceptional governor.

Finnuala Al Smith.

Moses A man of vision.

Finnuala Where I live, we call him one of us.

Moses Exactly. A man, like yourself, born into disadvantage. Brought up in the tenements. And therefore, like many such men, driven, purposeful.

Finnuala Oh, so you imagine deprivation is good for the character? I can assure you it isn't.

Moses Miss Connell, you're living proof that it is.

Finnuala is embarrassed. She becomes flustered.

Finnuala Well, I wouldn't know about that.

Moses I'm sorry –

Finnuala No –

Moses Forgive me –

Finnuala Nothing to forgive. I know you meant it as a pure compliment –

Moses I did –

Finnuala And I take it as such –

Moses Thank you. And that's why I'm so interested to hear your reports of the Governor's visits –

Finnuala Ah yes –

Moses When he drops by.

Finnuala You want to hear what he says?

Moses I do.

Finnuala And is that because you need the Governor? You need him on your side?

Moses Perhaps.

Moses looks, wondering freshly at her acuity.

Finnuala Am I right in thinking your fortunes are tied to his? And that if you didn't have Al Smith as your boss, the likelihood is, you wouldn't be able to do anything at all?

Moses says nothing, sulking.

Moses All right, I owe all advancement I have enjoyed to the Governor. I was languishing. He picked me out.

Finnuala How?

Moses We got on at once. He saw the point of me.

Finnuala Oh, did he?

Moses Yes.

Finnuala He's your patron?

Moses Sort of.

Finnuala You're in his debt?

Stubborn still, Moses won't answer.

As long as he's in office, you're in business.

Moses All right, that's a harsh way of putting it. But it's true.

He's irritated at having to admit it. Finnuala smiles to herself, and hums a little as she sets back to work. Moses is annoyed.

And what's put you in such a good mood?

Finnuala Oh, I'm thinking of going to the local store and buying a little flag.

Moses What sort of flag?

Finnuala A flag of commemoration.

Moses A commemoration? Of what?

Finnuala I think you know.

Moses No, I don't.

Finnuala Why, because it's the first time I've heard Robert Moses admit he needed someone else.

She's grinning as Porter and the junior draughtsmen return with their charts.

Moses Ah, Porter, good –

Porter We're back.

Moses You've done as I asked?

Porter We've restored the original route.

Moses Such an effort to get one's way. Especially with one's own employees. Is that not right, Miss Connell?

Finnuala I wouldn't know.

Moses Now let me see –

He goes to the table, every inch the master planner.

If everything is back in place, it looks to me there is no reason we should not proceed.

Porter Proceed?

Moses Yes.

Porter I'm sorry, sir, but I'm not sure what you mean by 'proceed'.

Moses I mean that the diggers can go in. There's nothing holding us back. Let the work begin.

Porter looks confused.

Why are you looking so doubtful?

Porter Just, it's my understanding – perhaps I'm misinformed – that there's a lawsuit that's outstanding against us.

Moses Yes, you're right.

Porter From the Taylor Estate. It claimed that you'd exceeded your authority.

Moses Correct.

Porter We were not meant to use our first allocation of money to appropriate land.

Moses And?

Porter You used it to appropriate land.

Moses You're well informed.

Porter is frightened but unyielding.

Porter Also –

Moses Yes?

Porter Again, maybe I'm in error here –

Moses I'm sure you're not, Porter, you seem to be a mine of unhelpful information –

Porter There's a question as to whether it's legal in the first place to appropriate land. Do we have that right?

Moses Use your spare time – if you have any, that is – reading Section 59 of the Conservation Law, passed by the US Congress in 1884. That should put your mind at rest. It deals with the question of appropriation.

He's playing to the gallery and his employees all laugh, enjoying Porter's discomfort. But Porter is not put off.

Porter Yes, but even if that particular legislation applies in this case – and that is at issue –

Moses So, you have read it –

Porter Even so, what *is* clear is that no project can be advanced without the Governor's signature.

Moses That's right.

Porter And it appears right now that you proceeded without it.

Moses waits.

Moses And therefore?

Porter And therefore, I'm just saying.

Moses You're just saying what?

Porter I'd imagined we'd be delaying construction until the case was settled. You know much better than me, but isn't that the law? Don't we have to delay? Until the appeal?

Moses smiles, tolerant.

Moses Porter, I'll tell you something about building.

Porter Please.

Moses Once you sink that first stake, they'll never make you pull it up. Public work relies on one thing.

Finnuala What's that?

Moses Impetus.

Porter But surely, we'll get into trouble, won't we? We'll be breaking the law.

Moses And that worries you?

Porter looks to the others for support, but they're keeping out of it.

Haussmann didn't give a straw for legality. He knocked down the greater part of Paris.

Porter That was a long time ago.

Moses Yes, and on a much larger scale.

Porter I'm concerned that if we proceed with laying tarmac, we shall be ordered to rip it back up. I'm not being pessimistic, sir –

Moses Good, I'm glad you're not pessimistic –

Porter But we lost in the first round –

Moses That was in a lower court –

Porter Yes –

Moses On the first hearing –

Porter And from what I'm told I'm not at all sure that the appeal will go our way.

Moses Really?

Porter No. I've got a cousin. He's a professional lawyer –

Moses Oh well then –

Porter He's worked in City Hall –

Moses Surely, he must be well connected –

Porter And he's been telling me that realistically the appeal could take a very long time.

Moses I'm doing everything I can to delay it –

Porter Delay it?

Moses Certainly.

Porter Why?

Moses Because the best way to deal with any lawsuit is to snarl it up in the courts.

Porter Is that wise? Isn't it better to get the thing settled?

Moses Why?

Porter Isn't it better to know? That way you have certainty.

Moses And certainty soothes you, does it?

Porter I'm just pointing out. My cousin implies that at the end victory is by no means assured.

Moses Does he say that?

Porter He's read the bill you drafted establishing the State Council of Parks, and he detects an element of –

Porter stops.

Moses An element of what, Porter?

Porter An element of legerdemain.

Moses Legerdemain?

Porter Yes. In the drafting. He's not sure the state legislators quite understood what they were agreeing to.

Moses If that's true, then the fault lies with them, not with me.

Moses sits back, expansive.

I pride myself on the drafting of legislation. It's one of my skills.

Porter Surely.

Moses I certainly aim to be adroit. In the clauses. In the wording.

Porter Adroit, yes.

Moses If you make things too explicit, too clear, when you draft a bill, then you may provoke unnecessary resistance. That's why a level of ambiguity is called for.

Porter I'm sure.

Moses I hope your cousin is not implying trickery.

Porter Oh no.

Moses Thank the Lord. My virtue's intact.

Porter But even so, he still thinks that at the end, on the final appeal, the case will be in the balance.

This time Moses is not annoyed, just amused. He turns, appealing to everyone else.

Moses Porter, you have a lot to learn.

Porter I know that, sir.

Moses If we all waited for litigation to be settled, we'd never do anything at all.

Porter I can see that, sir.

Moses Anyone can argue about where a freeway ought to be. But it's pretty damn hard to argue about where it is.

Porter So, what you're saying –

Moses I'm saying, you worry about the tarmac, I'll concern myself with the law. And if they put you in prison, I promise to visit weekly with apple cider and a baloney sandwich.

Everyone laughs obediently.

Porter Yes, sir. It's just –

He hesitates, nervous.

Moses Go on, Porter.

Porter It's just some of us here – we do read the papers on the way to work. Don't we?

He appeals, but nobody helps.

And although you haven't mentioned it – nobody's mentioned it in the office – it's never come up in discussion – nevertheless –

Moses Yes, Porter?

Porter When the court found us guilty of illegal appropriation –

Moses Yes?

Porter We couldn't help noticing that you yourself, sir, were personally fined twenty-two thousand dollars in punitive damages.

Moses So?

Porter I hope that was correctly reported.

Moses It was.

He waits.

Well?

He waits.

Well?

Porter Are you proposing to pay? I'm not being selfish, sir, but if you don't pay that fine, you go to jail, and we're all out of a job.

Moses turns, vigorous, reanimated.

Moses Is there no fight in us, Porter? Is there no joy? Do you not wake up every morning with the feeling that what we're doing is good? Does that not sustain you? The incorruptible pleasure of being right? Liberating the land and handing it to the people. If that's an offence, then it's an offence to be alive.

SIX

Finnuala steps out of the scene and speaks directly to us.

Finnuala And that's how it was, working for him. Like you were on horseback and galloping across the plain.

He'd been told by his mother that he was going to excel, so for him there was no doubt about it.

It was his mother who told him he wasn't Jewish, so as far as Robert was concerned, he wasn't. He preferred to identify with the Protestants. He didn't care to be a Jew.

If someone said, 'But your name is Moses,' he'd reply, 'I'll show you my pecker. There, does that settle the matter?'

But if you're wondering, he never showed it to me.

SEVEN

Jacobs returns, at the other side.

Jacobs You could say my problems had started before the Second World War. I was a journalist, I was writing for a downtown magazine called *Iron Age*. It was specialised. You could write about iron or you could write about steel.

So the problem was this: I found I was being paid less than the men in the office who did the same job. Quite a lot less. So I decided to join a union and fight for my rights.

Eventually, I got my money but, in the process, I destroyed the atmosphere at *Iron Age*. Unintentionally, thanks to me, it ceased to be a pleasant place to work.

If you think fighting power is fun, I'd advise you to think again.

I knew that already when I went to war with Bob Moses.

EIGHT

Porter and Finnuala are working quietly at draughtsman's tables when the door opens and Governor Al Smith bursts in. He is in his fifties, short, red-faced, blue-eyed, with a wide-striped suit and a bowler hat. The dining room has become even more overwhelmed with architect's plans – it is groaning with papers, drawings, noticeboards.

Smith Where is he? Where is the son of a bitch? Don't say he's out romancing the shore? Will somebody tell him it's just a beach? It's a fucking beach.

Smith turns to address Finnuala.

And you're fucking Irish, I know you are, so I don't have to fake an apology which doesn't come from my black Fenian heart.

Terrified, Porter and Finnuala have got up, like animals, not sure where to go. A couple of other young draughtsmen have appeared, equally scared, at the door.

Finnuala People have used profanity around me all my life.

Smith You talking about your family?

Finnuala They use that word.

Smith Then you're inoculated.

Finnuala More than. My cousins curse every time they breathe.

Smith Do they indeed?

Finnuala At lunch, at dinner, when they go to bed, when they fall over their shoelaces, and when they go to church.

Smith Inside the church?

Finnuala Certainly.

Smith In the presence of a priest?

Finnuala I'm afraid so.

Smith Tell your cousins they only get five for a priest. You get ten for a nun.

Porter I'm going looking.

Porter has vanished out the door in search of Moses.

Smith Have you met Franklin Roosevelt?

Finnuala No.

Smith Franklin D.? He doesn't curse. And that's all you need to know about the upstate motherfucker.

Finnuala I've heard that, yes.

Smith He's head of the Boy Scout movement. Did you know that?

Finnuala I didn't, actually.

Smith That and his stuck-up wife. Looking down their aristocratic noses at a Mick from the fourth ward.

Finnuala That would be you, would it, sir?

Smith And proud of it.

Smith is now looking at the boards on the wall.

What the hell is all this?

Finnuala Drawings.

Smith Every time I visit, the plans are further progressed.

Finnuala Yes. We've begun building the parkway.

Smith I beg your pardon, young lady?

Finnuala We've begun building.

Smith Impossible.

Finnuala We've started.

Smith Which Parkway? South Parkway or North?

Finnuala Both.

Smith That's the first I've heard of it.

Finnuala Oh.

Smith I don't see how you can have started because I haven't signed. I haven't signed the fucking legislation.

Smith stares at her, waiting for a response.

Finnuala Then perhaps that's something you'll have to discuss with Mr Moses?

Smith Indeed, I will.

Finnuala Forget I spoke.

Smith I can't forget. Fuck! Someone tell me: is that man at it again?

Porter has reappeared anxious at the door.

Porter He can't be found.

Smith Then where is he?

Finnuala Did you tell him you were coming?

Smith I don't tell him. I like to catch the bastard off guard.

Porter Do you want me to send out a search party?

Smith What's he doing? Diddling in the water? Or pacing out a block of Theban shithouses for twenty thousand holiday makers?

Porter One or two of the guys have been wondering if there's anything we can get you, Governor.

Smith Why not break the law and serve me a bottle of bourbon?

Porter Funny, we guessed that.

He looks relieved and goes out again. Smith lights a cigar and smiles at Finnuala.

Smith As if I gave a fuck about parks.

Finnuala Don't you, sir?

Smith Look at me. Do I look like someone who hangs around parks?

Finnuala No.

Smith I'm not that sad. I've better things to do with my time. I've never lifted a hiking boot in anger in my life.

Finnuala It hasn't done you any harm.

Smith Thank you.

Finnuala You look well on it, Governor.

Smith I'm five minutes shy of cardiac arrest, I know that, so don't soap me. It's the voters who like parks, not me.

Finnuala And you care about the voters, surely?

Smith The lower-class people, they like parks. And so do the middle. So that's two handy groups with a lot of votes between them.

Finnuala Indeed.

Smith And the intellectuals, oh sure, they love parks because they think parks are progressive, fuck knows why.

Finnuala Maybe they feel it's progress towards a better life.

Smith Maybe.

Finnuala That's certainly what Mr Moses believes.

Smith considers her a moment.

Smith You like him, don't you?

Finnuala Who's that?

Smith Your boss.

Finnuala I neither like nor dislike him. I keep personal feelings out of it.

Smith Are you kidding me?

Finnuala He's on the side of the angels, that's what matters.

Smith On the side of the angels, and using the methods of the devil.

Finnuala He's starting to get things done.

Smith Then you like him.

Finnuala I like him enough.

Smith You're lucky because he doesn't need anything from you. That's when he plays you like a fish. 'Governor, this. Governor, that.' When I leave the room, I look to see if my fob is still in my pocket.

Finnuala shrugs slightly, as if to say that's not important.

52

Finnuala Well if you'll allow me, I've never once heard him say a word against you.

Smith Is that so?

Finnuala Never.

Smith Behind my back?

Finnuala He says politicians are all the same. All frightened. He has contempt for them. That's why he's not interested in elective office.

Smith No, I'm sure he's not.

Finnuala But you're different. He says you're the only politician who's for real.

Smith is pleased with the flattery, but also a touch suspicious.

Smith Does he say that?

Finnuala He does.

Smith Spontaneous, like?

Finnuala He respects you.

Smith And what do you imagine would be the reason for that, Miss Connell? I'll tell you. Because he feels if he lays the butter on thick enough, he can wangle anything he wants from an ignorant Mick.

Finnuala No.

Smith Why then?

Finnuala He feels you're not in it for personal glory, but because you came from the streets yourself and you love the people of New York.

Porter returns with the bottle. Smith, susceptible to her sincerity, covers up his pleasure in what she just said.

Smith Maybe. But I love bourbon more.

Finnuala You have it.

Porter He keeps the bottle for you.

Smith I'm sure he does.

Porter He says the bootleg is top class.

Smith Thank you. You're a good boy.

Smith nods approval of the brand.

Smith So what about you? What's your view of your boss?

Porter Me, sir?

Smith Yes, you. I've forgotten your name.

Porter Ariel Porter.

Smith Ariel?

Porter Yes.

Smith What kind of name is that?

Porter It's a Hebrew name, sir. Meaning 'lion of God'.

Smith Who gave you that name?

Porter My father.

Smith Where are you from?

Porter Oklahoma.

Smith finds this amusing.

Smith Many Jews in Oklahoma, are there?

Porter No, sir. We strayed off-track.

Smith And what feelings do you have towards Robert Moses?

Porter I feel he's a visionary.

Smith Visionary's a big word, Porter.

Porter He's lifting the people up and giving them the opportunity for a kind of freedom they've never had before.

Smith Is that right?

Porter The *New York Times* is an important newspaper.

Smith You think so?

Porter Oh, I do. It's read by some of the most influential people on the planet.

Smith So they tell me.

Porter And yet somehow Mr Moses has them eating out his hand. Reporters love him.

Smith They do indeed. He knows what they want and he gives it to them. You might even say that's where his real genius lies. He's a new kind of man, Mr Moses. The man who believes that the way you're written about is as important as what you do.

Smith's tone is sarcastic, but Porter doesn't notice.

Porter All I can say: it's a privilege to come to work every day.

Smith A privilege, is it?

Porter Oh, I can see he's controversial, and maybe he doesn't treat the law with the respect we learned at school, but it's only once in a generation that a great builder comes along and shows the way. That's when you're party to a vision that's denied to ordinary men.

Smith And you're party to that vision, are you?

Porter Yes, sir. In some humble way.

Smith I wonder, have you ever heard the saying that it's easier to be a great man than it is to be a good man?

Porter No, I've never heard that.

Smith You've heard it now.

Porter I like the sentiment.

Smith Yes, I like it too.

Smith has poured himself a large bourbon.

And tell me, when the boy from Oklahoma arrives at work in the morning, are you frightened of the great builder?

Porter Frightened?

Smith Yes.

Porter looks anxiously to Finnuala as if she could help.

Well?

Porter To be honest –

Smith Be honest –

Porter Absolutely scared out of my skin.

Moses arrives, apparently fresh from the sea. He has a shirt, shorts, and a towel round his neck.

Moses For Christ's sake, Porter, don't you know not to give the Governor bourbon?

Smith Moses, where the hell have you been?

Moses Do you have no sense? The Governor's wife went down on her knees to me, on the carpet – *on the carpet –* begging me, saying whatever you do, don't let Al near the hooch.

Smith And this bare-faced liar in five minutes will be asking me for favours.

Moses I never ask favours. I ask my due.

Smith And I'll tell you one thing: he's barely spoken to my wife in his life.

Moses We speak all the time.

Smith I don't think so.

Moses She says, 'Give him soda water. And one an hour, on the hour, at the very most.'

Smith My wife can't stand him.

Moses Catherine worships me.

Smith Come here, you dog.

The two men embrace. It's love – the intellectual and the street fighter.

Moses And while I was swimming in the brine, the Governor was swimming in bootleg whiskey, to judge from the smell of him. Pure rye.

Smith And after the day I've had, why would that not be so?

Moses You're complaining, are you?

Smith You'd be complaining in my shoes.

Moses Running the greatest city in the world, in the greatest state in the world? I'd be complaining? I don't think so.

Smith So you want my job, do you?

Moses Do I want it?

Smith Do you want to be Governor?

Moses Why, Al, tell me when the bus is coming and I'll be there to push you under it.

Smith You'll join the fucking line.

The two men laugh. It's a routine and they love it.

Moses Obviously, Governor, you know my team?

Smith I believe I do.

Moses Finnuala, Ariel . . .

Smith I've come upon them once or twice.

Moses Of course you have. They tell me you visit occasionally when I'm not here.

Smith I do indeed.

Moses Dropping by. To sneak a look at the plans.

Smith ignores him.

Smith I admire young people.

Moses They're hand-picked.

Smith And are they as crazy as you about causeways and parkways and expressways and all the other ways?

Moses They are now. I've taught them to serve the public, and free the people from ugliness and squalor. To give them a view of something better than the animal cages in which they live.

Smith is sitting down with his bourbon.

Porter We'll leave you alone.

Smith No, stay with us.

Finnuala Are you sure, sir?

Smith Do you mind, Bob?

Moses Not at all. Let them stay. It's good for them to learn the practical stuff, if that's what you're suggesting, Governor. One day or another, we all have to learn how the thing is done.

Smith Perhaps we do.

Moses They'll learn by listening.

Smith But are you sure that you yourself, Bob, have ever learned how the thing is done?

Moses Me?

Smith You, Bob. Yes.

Smith's tone has suddenly changed.

Moses What makes you ask that?

Smith looks at him hard, then turns away.

Smith I'm about to fight a fucking election, remember?

Moses So you are.

Smith A close election in which every vote is going to count. Do you know what that means? I have to crawl down the sidewalk on my hands and knees, begging people to like me.

Moses They do like you, Governor.

Smith Sure. But it's not an indignity you've ever had to endure.

Smith turns to the others.

You see, your boss is far too grand to get himself involved in the vulgar business of getting elected.

Moses I've never tried, no.

Smith He never has.

Moses I've never had to.

Smith He gets other people to stand for election on his behalf.

Moses has sat down at the end of the big table. Smith is prowling, glass in hand. The young ones are nervous.

Moses Governor, that isn't quite the way it is.

Smith Wouldn't take the risk, is another way of putting it.

Moses I'm not against risk.

Smith Aren't you?

Moses Just: standing for public office, that's not my specialty.

59

Smith An election's a terrible sort of judgement, you know. A judgement on a man's character. No way of getting around it. It's frightening.

Moses I'm sure it is.

Smith You ask so many million people what they think of you. Imagine that.

Moses tries to make a joke of it.

Moses That's why I'd rather not, thank you.

Smith And you're not always going to like the fucking answer.

Moses shifts, not sure where Smith is going.

Moses Come on, Governor, what's this about? You've won more elections than any man alive. How many times have you run for public office?

Smith I'm thinking it's probably nineteen.

Moses You don't know exactly?

Smith It's nineteen.

Moses And how many times have you won?

Smith Nineteen.

Moses Well, there you are.

Everyone laughs and applauds, Moses winks at the team, but Smith is not put off.

Smith You see, that's the difference between Bob and me. Your Mr Moses doesn't like to fight for power. He prefers to let others acquire it for him.

Moses looks round a moment, not rising to the bait.

With Mr Moses, it's always the same.

Moses In what way is it the same, exactly?

Smith He goes after what he wants.

Moses So do you, Governor.

Smith And making enemies doesn't bother him. He feels free to go around making as many enemies as he chooses.

Moses shrugs.

Moses I don't make them deliberately.

Smith Don't you?

Moses No.

Smith It's my experience that if your boss sees someone on the other side of the street, he can't resist crossing that street to tell them they're a son of a bitch.

Moses I don't think I've ever done that.

Smith And shall I tell you why he does it? Because he knows he always has someone at hand who's there to clear up the mess.

Finnuala And who is that person, Governor?

Smith Why that would be me, Miss Connell.

Moses stares, uneasy.

Porter Are you sure you want us to be here?

Moses Quite sure.

Nobody moves. Smith is gaining purpose now.

Smith You see, I've been in politics for a while, and I'll tell you how things usually go. The boss is usually the public face. He has to answer many questions on many subjects. And it's for that reason the boss has a team, and I'll tell you what their job is. Their job is to put right the things the boss, in his haste or ignorance, got wrong.

Smith stops. He shrugs.

Only tell you something, it's odd, when you have Robert Moses on the staff, the situation is reversed. Moses fucks up and the boss's job is to clean up the mess.

Smith's geniality has turned into real ferocity. Moses looks sulky, dark.

Moses I wasn't aware I'd fucked up, as you put it.

Smith Weren't you?

Moses No.

Smith The lawsuit?

Moses An inconvenience, Governor, not a fuck-up. It hasn't shaken me –

Smith No, I noticed –

Moses I'm sure we'll win in a superior court.

Smith Will we?

Moses Eventually.

Smith If someone gives you the money to get there. Isn't that what you rely on? The state has bottomless pockets, the individual doesn't? You're hoping to wear your enemy down, is that it, with the financial support of New York State?

Neither of them moves. Moses is careful.

Moses Forgive me if I'm in error, but I've always had the impression you were going to back me.

Smith Where did you get that impression, Bob?

Moses You want these state parks and parkways as badly as I do.

Smith Do I?

Moses Why, sure you do.

Smith For your own sake, you'd better be right about that.

Moses I believe I am.

Smith You wouldn't be taking me for granted, would you?

Smith laughs. Moses is discomforted.

Again, a lot of people talk to me, they like to talk to me, in the streets, in the barber's shop, hell, they talk to me in the Turkish bath, because I'm approachable –

Moses You certainly are –

Smith The rumour I've heard is that your mother has paid your personal fine. Is that true?

Smith waits.

Tell me. Did your mother step up for her little boy?

Moses It isn't strictly your business, Governor, is it?

Smith Not my business, eh?

Moses It was a personal fine. I dealt with it personally.

Smith Meaning your dear mama has covered it?

Moses It's not your business.

Moses is looking daggers at him. Smith turns again to Finnuala and Porter.

Smith That's one of your boss's virtues, team. You could call it a mark of honour that he doesn't even have the money to pay his own fine. Whatever you may say about him – and believe me, I say plenty – he's not on the take. He has family to reach in their pockets for him.

Moses On this occasion only.

Smith Good.

Moses It happened once.

Smith laughs, gaining force now.

Smith Because, just remind me – I'm relying on my memory here and it isn't always accurate – the reason you found yourself in court was because you went ahead and seized private land for some park without the Governor's signature?

Moses I didn't seize it, I bought it.

Smith At less than the market rate.

Moses So the owner claims.

Smith It was the Taylor Estate.

Moses We both know: it was a technical offence –

Smith Technical?

Moses Yes.

Smith Purely technical?

Moses It was a matter of timing. You were going to sign, but you hadn't – at the moment of appropriation –

Smith How did you know I was going to sign it?

Moses I had a fair idea.

Smith In fact, you hadn't asked me –

Moses Correct –

Smith You hadn't even approached me –

Moses Correct –

Smith At that moment –

Moses It had slipped my mind. Perhaps I didn't know I needed the specific permission, Al.

Smith Perhaps.

Smith smiles.

Except – tell you something funny – I came here today, and I was just staring around the room, as you do, when your mind's wandering, making conversation with this delightful helpmate of yours, and there I was, staring at the Northern State Parkway –

Moses Ah yes –

Smith The plans on the boards –

Moses There they are –

Smith And I had a question for my young compatriot –

Moses And how did she answer?

Finnuala Mr Moses, I'm sorry I shouldn't have spoken –

Moses holds up a hand.

Moses No. Not your fault.

Finnuala I shouldn't.

Moses Whatever you said –

Smith Miss Connell told me the truth. As I would expect her to.

Moses I would expect that also.

Smith And she told me you'd started building not just one new parkway, but two.

Finnuala I did say that.

Smith You hadn't waited for my permission. You'd just sent the fucking diggers in. And not just to one highway, either. To two!

Moses says nothing.

And so it seems incredible to me that I once wanted to put in charge of prisons someone who doesn't know the meaning of the words 'repeat offender'.

Moses I do know their meaning, Governor.

Smith Well then.

Moses I just don't recognise myself in the description.

Smith Do not take me for a fucking idiot!

Smith has suddenly shouted.

Moses Governor, I have the greatest respect for you.

Smith Jesus Christ, Moses, if this is how you treat the people you respect, I dread to think how you treat the people you despise. Which, as I see it, is more or less the rest of the human race. None of them coming up to your standards of brilliance and fucking intellect!

Smith shouts again.

You lost the fucking case!

Moses Not yet.

Smith You lost it!

Moses It's going to appeal.

Smith And now you're charging ahead again with yet more appropriations which are illegal and unauthorised. You believe your brain can get you out of every situation your ego gets you into. Every family in Long Island wants to hang you from a lamp post upside down.

Moses And this bothers you, does it?

Smith It fucking well does. They're voters, just like everyone else.

Moses That's a problem for you, is it? The Mick from the Fourth Ward cares about the Vanderbilts, does he? He cares about the Whitneys? He cares about J. P. Morgans? Because my impression, Governor, is that they're not going to vote for you anyway. So what does it matter if we anger a few plutocrats who were never on our side in the first place?

Smith Because they have influence, that's why.

Moses Influence with who?

He waits. Then he shouts back.

I'm asking, Governor. Influence with who?

Smith jabs an angry finger at him.

Smith If you want a word of advice: leave the politics to me, you're tone fucking deaf to it. You get on with building.

Moses God in heaven, Governor, that's what I'm trying to do. Just sometimes you make it hard for me.

Smith I make it hard? I don't think so. You make it hard for yourself.

The atmosphere is now so rank that both Finnuala and Porter shift, uneasy, wanting to get out.

Finnuala I've got some urgent work –

Porter Me too –

Finnuala I need to attend to.

Smith I don't want you to do that, Miss Connell.

Finnuala I would like to be excused.

Smith Nothing you have in hand could be as important as what you are about to hear.

Moses And what is that?

Smith Mr Moses backing down. Mr Moses telling me he's going to obey me in future.

There is a deadly silence.

Moses And you hog the bourbon to yourself, do you?

Smith No, have some. Give some to your friends.

Porter No.

Finnuala No, thank you.

Moses gets three more glasses and pours, as from a tap.

Moses Drink, for Christ's sake, drink. Get into the spirit of the meeting.

He lifts his glass. Porter and Finnuala follow suit, nervously.

Here's to you, Governor.

Porter To you.

Finnuala To you.

They all drink. Moses nods, appreciative. Smith says nothing.

Moses You say to ignore the politics.

Smith Yes.

Moses But the building *is* the politics. I'm handing you a popular cause. My advice would be this: run with it.

Smith I'll run with the cause – the cause is fresh air, even if I hate the stuff myself – but I won't run with your methods. I won't. You're breaking the law.

Moses I'm in a hurry, and I'm in a hurry to help – to help the millions out there who have no access to a good life. And if a few fences get kicked over in the process, does that really matter? Please.

Smith is muted, mistrustful, as if he fears Moses is right.

Smith So what do you suggest?

Moses I suggest you appear in court. On my behalf.

Smith Are you out of your head?

Moses I don't think so.

Smith Governors never appear in courts. Never.

Moses I know.

Smith It's unheard of.

Moses Yes. That's why I want you to do it.

Moses smiles, suddenly confident.

In three weeks, we have a hearing. An appeal.

Smith Where?

Moses Riverhead.

Smith That's at the end of Long Island.

Moses I suggest you gather together a posse of reporters –

Smith Including the *New York Times*, no doubt?

Moses Never forgetting the *Times*.

Smith Naturally.

Moses And you all travel together, all friendly, all chatting, so that there's plenty of publicity when the previously unknown happens.

Smith Who's the judge?

Moses And that's the point of it. The appeal hearing is in front of Justice Dunne.

Smith James Dunne, eh?

Moses I believe you're already friends.

Smith We know each other, yes –

Moses I believe you play cards –

Smith From time to time –

Moses At your club.

Smith Poker.

A short silence.

Moses Dunne is going to be flattered to see you in his court.

Smith It's true. He will.

Moses And then maybe afterwards you might take him to lunch. Seeing that you're well acquainted. And both have an appetite around noon.

Silence. Finnuala and Porter are watching like hawks.

Smith And if I did that, what argument would I be making?

Moses spreads his hands as if to say 'Fait accompli'.

Moses It's pointless to dispute whether the Taylor Estate is or isn't a park. Because if he goes there, Justice Dunne will find picnic tables, he will find changing rooms, and he will find children from the slums playing contentedly in the sun. And given that the facilities have been provided and that, all summer long, visitors have been enjoying the place, does he really want to go down in history as the judge who stole a park from the people of New York? Does he want that mark against his name?

Smith nods, judicious.

Smith And so, tell me, please, if that's the line of argument –

Moses It is –

Smith If that's our case –

Moses In a nutshell –

Smith 'The park already exists, why take it away?'

Moses That's the case –

Smith Then I suppose I would want to know why it would be me having to make it, rather than you.

Moses shrugs.

Moses Obvious. Because it can't be said in the court.

Smith But it can be said in private over lunch?

Moses Just so. Also –

Moses hesitates.

Smith Yes?

Moses I make no secret of this. I'm a bad witness.

Smith Really?

Moses On the stand. When I had to appear, it was not advantageous.

Smith Why not?

Moses is still for a moment.

Moses It's as you say. People take against me.

Smith What people?

Moses Everyone in the court.

Smith Why?

Moses Something in my manner.

Smith What sort of thing?

Moses They think I'm arrogant.

Smith What on earth would make them think that?

Moses You're likeable. I'm not.

Smith runs his finger thoughtfully round the rim of his glass.

Smith Well, that's a hell of a thing for any man to say.

Moses I've said it.

Smith Many men may think it, but it's rare to say it.

Moses There we are.

Smith And to say it in front of your juniors is even rarer.

Moses I have no secrets from them. I make a poor impression in court. It's not my natural field of operation.

Moses suddenly leans forward.

If you can swing this thing, Al, if you can charm that judge, then you have my word, you will have cleared your path to your re-election. And I don't know any right-thinking man in the state of New York who won't throw their hat in the air when that happens.

Smith nods, thoughtful.

Smith I'm going to think about this.

Moses Good.

Smith I'm going to think about what you suggest.

Moses That's kind of you, Governor. Thank you. We're in your debt.

Smith pushes his glass away, then gets up as if to leave. But before he goes, he turns back.

Smith Oh yeah. One other thing, I nearly forgot.

Moses Anything.

Smith The train.

Moses The train?

Smith Yeah. The train to Jones Beach. Remember?

Moses Yes, of course.

Smith When you open up your beautiful beach, your masterpiece, you'll need to provide public transportation. How are the plans coming on?

Moses They're embryonic.

Smith You'll have to say that again.

Moses They're advancing.

Smith Good.

Moses pauses a second.

Moses But I still imagine the majority of people arriving by car.

Smith I'm sure you do.

Moses Governor, the car is the future. I believe in the motor car.

Smith Yes, but I'm talking about poor people, Bob. The people who can't afford cars. Coloured people, Bob. Hispanics. How will they get to the beach?

Moses People want to travel alone. Not to have to suffer other people's mess and noise.

Smith Some people don't have a choice. You don't come from the workers. I do. And I know what they like. They like mess and noise, Bob. They think mess and noise are life.

Moses I think you'll find the majority prefer to go under their own steam. In their own contained space.

Smith I want a train. I want my voters on this beach. All of them.

Moses looks him in the eye.

It's an order. Trains, buses and cars. All three. Or no beach.

Moses I'll bear that in mind.

Moses gets up.

Smith Give my regards to Mary.

Moses I certainly will.

Smith Are you taking enough care? There are times I wonder if you take enough care of her.

Moses I promise I do.

Smith Good.

Moses Porter will see you on your way.

Porter It'll be a privilege.

Moses And thank you, Governor.

Smith Hard to leave a meeting with Moses without feeling you've been robbed. But just as hard to know what the fuck you've been robbed of. Goodbye, everyone.

Smith goes out with Porter. Finnuala starts to tidy up the glasses and bottle.

Moses Well, that went off as well as we could have hoped.

Finnuala says nothing.

What's the sour mood?

Finnuala I'm not sour.

Moses You are sour. Why?

Finnuala Because specifically yesterday you said no train.

Moses I did say that. And, yes, I'm still saying that. And I'll continue to say that, whatever the Governor requests. You work for me, Finnuala, not for him. Do you have a problem with that?

Finnuala says nothing.

I want a clean beach. I want an unspoilt beach.

Finnuala Unspoilt?

Moses I want a non-commercial beach.

Finnuala turns and looks at him.

Finnuala So let me get this straight. We're building a beach for the masses. Correct? But the masses won't be able to get there by train, and if we stick to the current plans, you're not even giving access for buses. So remind me, which masses exactly is this beach for?

Moses They arrive by car.

Finnuala And the people who can't afford a car?

Moses looks at her with mixture of fondness and condescension.

Moses Don't you start, Finnuala. Don't you start doubting.

NINE

Finnuala steps out of the scene and talks directly to us. Behind her, countless cars in a 1930s traffic jam, at a standstill, bumper to bumper, making for the beach.

Finnuala And that's how we began. Al Smith took the judge out to lunch.

Today, if a person is driving on a road anywhere in New York State which has the word 'expressway' in its name, they are driving on a road built by Robert Moses.

Eventually, we would build six hundred and twenty-seven miles of highway.

But we never built a train to Jones Beach.

TEN

Jacobs appears. Behind her, the architectural plans for a highway sweeping down from Fifth Avenue through Lower Manhattan.

Jacobs Early in the fifties, I moved from *Iron Age* to *Architectural Forum*.

I hadn't taken much notice of Robert Moses. I only knew what everyone knew: that he was straight line crazy.

Like most architects, he wanted to put a straight line between any two points and build where his ruler went.

So now he drew a line for an expressway straight down the middle of the city.

By then, he'd encircled Manhattan with bridges and roads. So the moment had come to rip through Manhattan itself.

End of Act One.

Act Two

ELEVEN

Music, deep, romantic. A public meeting in Greenwich Village, attended by residents. It's 1955. At a table are the chairwoman, Shirley Hayes, forties; Sandy McQuade, an architectural critic, thirty-three; Lewis Mason, sixty, a grand old man of urban planning; a young black activist, Carol Amis; and Nicole Savage, forties, a gallery owner. Hayes is introducing Jacobs, forty, also at the table. Behind them, an idyllic image of the Square – shady, with abundant trees, children, chess players, etc.

Hayes The next speaker is a friend of ours. She's lived in the Village for many, many years – it's her home, as it's been mine, for a long time, she lives on Hudson – a friend said of her 'What a dear, sweet character she isn't' – and she's writing a book about – well, it's not for me to say, you tell us, Jane –

Jacobs Kind of city things.

Hayes There it is, kind of city things –

Jacobs What is a city? What should it be? Why do we live in groups? What do we want from cities? And who decides?

Hayes Jane knows everything and the one thing she really knows is, she sure as hell doesn't want a road straight through Washington Square Park.

Applause.

Jane.

Jacobs gets up, blinking.

Jacobs What I do know: cities grow up. They just happen. Bit by bit. Hand a city to the planners and they'll make it a desert. Hand it to the people and they'll make it habitable.

77

Robert Moses looks at the West Village and he sees a slum. I look at the West Village and I see a healthy neighbourhood. I see life.

Applause.

Bob Moses loves government. I don't. I don't trust it. In the last twenty-five years, Moses has moved two hundred and fifty thousand people out of their homes to make way for his roads, and he's built lifeless slabs. The people who live in them hate them. You can build ovens, but you can't expect the loaves to jump in.

Wilder applause and cheers.

I don't understand why it's progress to destroy things people love. And if you're thinking I'm too sure of myself, I can only say you're right. Yes, I am sure of myself. But unlike Robert Moses, I'm not full of myself.

More applause.

We need war, full out and flat out, to stop this hideous violation which Moses is planning. He just destroyed the Bronx, now he wants to destroy the Village. People say don't fight dirty, that's what the enemy does. But I say if the fight's in the mud, then it's into the mud we go and it's in the mud we win.

TWELVE

1955. The Headquarters of the Triborough Bridge Authority on Randall's Island. A purpose-built office building just below the Toll Plaza. Moses' office is imperial. On shelves, the evidence of countless projects. There is a large central desk, and a side-table where Finnuala is working. She is in her early fifties, as neat and tidy as ever. Mariah Heller, a tidy and efficient black American, twenties, comes in, carrying bundles of files.

Finnuala Is he back?

Heller No sign of him.

Finnuala Lunch with the Mayor. It's always endless. He can't get away.

Heller It's quarter to four.

Finnuala That's lunch for you. Robert Wagner makes him drink Martinis which he hates. And then Wagner talks for ever.

Heller Mr Moses hates everyone in authority, doesn't he?

Finnuala He didn't hate Al Smith. He worshipped him.

Heller frowns.

Heller I'm sorry to ask this –

Finnuala It's okay –

Heller But just remind me.

Finnuala Mr Smith was Mr Moses' first Governor. Thirty years ago.

Heller Is that the Al Smith who ran for president?

Finnuala Yes.

Heller When was that?

Finnuala In 1928.

Heller I wasn't born.

Finnuala He was unsuccessful.

Heller Why did he lose?

Finnuala He was a Catholic.

Heller You think a Catholic can never be president?

Finnuala All I can tell you: it's the only election Al Smith ever lost.

Finnuala smiles.

Mr Moses says when it comes to politicians, Smith's the only one he ever worked for. All the others he worked in spite of.

Heller That's funny.

Finnuala He still calls him Governor. He died in 1944.

Heller Why was he so fond of him?

Finnuala Similar kind of personality, maybe.

Heller Was Mr Smith a bully?

Finnuala Is that how you characterise Mr Moses?

Heller hesitates.

It's all right. You can say anything you like. I promise it won't get back to him.

Heller hesitates, thinking.

Heller I guess Mr Moses is a man who's used to getting his own way. He's very sure of his own ideas.

Finnuala And you don't agree with them?

Heller Oh, look, Miss Connell, I'm starting out. I'm just out of school. I've never practised architecture.

Finnuala But?

Heller shrugs, embarrassed.

Heller Okay, well, since you ask, it is all a little disappointing.

Finnuala Why?

Heller At school we were all on fire about Walter Gropius and Le Corbusier – you know about them?

Finnuala I do.

Heller Sorry, of course you do – Bauhaus – people wanting to make architecture modern –

Finnuala It's an exciting time –

Heller Sure is –

Finnuala To be a student –

Heller The sky's the limit. And when I got my first job helping out here – look, I know what a pioneer Mr Moses is, New York wouldn't be New York without him, the road system, the West Side Highway, and there he is all over the state –

Finnuala He is indeed –

Heller The parks, the playgrounds, the swimming pools –

Finnuala Sure –

Heller The bridges, the housing schemes, getting the UN for New York, everything – there's never been anything like it – the scale – but it's just working with him, I am surprised.

Finnuala Are you? In what way?

Heller I was expecting an exchange of ideas.

Finnuala is silent for a moment.

Finnuala Okay.

Heller I know I'm the lowest of the low –

Finnuala Not quite –

Heller But I haven't heard much stuff being bounced around.

Finnuala It's true. With Bob, there's not a lot of bouncing around.

Heller Also, it's complicated. I had family who lived in the Bronx.

Finnuala looks up.

Finnuala Okay. You've never mentioned them.

Heller No.

Finnuala Close family?

Heller Uncles. Aunts. Cousins. They got moved out. To make way for the Cross-Bronx Expressway. Only that's not what my family call it.

Finnuala What's their name for it?

Heller They call it the Heartbreak Highway. And now they're fifteen miles out, way beyond Queens. So I don't go round telling everyone where I work.

Finnuala I understand.

Heller I've only been here eight months – I'm pretty sure it was you who wanted me for the job, not him – but I've never once known him to change his mind.

Finnuala No.

Heller About anything. Does he ever?

Finnuala looks at her, not wanting to concede.

From what I've heard, if you disagree with him, you don't last very long.

Finnuala That's not fair.

Heller Are you saying it isn't true?

Finnuala Mr Moses has built an awful lot of stuff. That means he's encountered an awful lot of opposition. That's tiring. It can make you a bit scratchy.

Heller Sure.

Finnuala Somebody has to lead. It's impossible to plan things by committee. I don't believe anyone ever called your Mr Corbusier flexible.

82

Heller No. But Corbusier contacts people and keeps in touch with how they live.

Finnuala And you feel Mr Moses doesn't?

Heller looks at her a moment.

Heller You know him better than me.

Finnuala Yeah.

Heller You wouldn't have spent your whole life with him, would you, unless you saw his virtues?

Finnuala looks at her a moment.

Finnuala No, I wouldn't, would I?

Heller hears the sadness in her voice. Finnuala gets up from her desk, pulling her cardigan tighter, as though she were chilly. She refreshes her mug of tea with hot water.

Heller Mr Porter says he's never heard you say a word against him.

Finnuala When we argue, it's behind closed doors.

Heller Did you never work for anyone else?

Finnuala shakes her head.

Did you never want to?

Finnuala Oh, sure I did. I would like to have been an architect myself. But it didn't pan out. Like a lot of things. You know?

Heller doesn't, but she waits, respectful.

Finnuala Apart from anything, there was the Crash. If you had a paying job, you held on to it.

Heller That was a long time ago.

Finnuala Even after the Depression was over, the mindset remained. Inevitably. That kind of experience marks you.

Finnuala turns and looks at her.

Also, I got waylaid by personal misfortune. There you are.

She goes and sits at her desk, resumes her work. Heller is left puzzled.

Heller But you don't regret spending your whole life here?

Finnuala One thing working here: there's always excitement.

Heller And at the end of it?

Finnuala Oh, let's hope it's not the end yet.

Moses comes in, now in his sixties, in Oxford dress shirt with cufflinks, suit, dark tie, gaunter but as turbulent as ever. He throws down his coat.

Moses And if someone can tell me what the point of lunch is, I'd love to know.

Finnuala You're happy enough to lunch when you're the host.

Moses I hate it when I'm a guest.

Finnuala You like to be in control.

Finnuala gets up to get him water. It's a well-oiled routine.

Moses And I despise the 21 Club. Manhattan's smug elite, eating hamburgers and pretending to be European. Forget that.

Finnuala Do you want the Pepto-Bismol?

Moses Urgently.

Finnuala It's coming.

She gets some from under the desk.

Did you drink?

Moses A Martini. To be sociable. I left most of it. The Mayor had three. I see enough drinking at home.

Finnuala I know.

He looks at her a moment.

Moses And Caesar salad? What is that? Lettuce coated with slime –

Finnuala You really had a good time, didn't you?

Moses doesn't reply.

Liquid or tablet?

Moses Both.

Moses has taken his jacket off, and is at his desk. He looks up at Heller, who has not moved from the side of the room, files still under her arm.

The Mayor works the room. He says hello to the party in each booth. It's like having lunch with a hooker.

Finnuala You wouldn't do that?

Moses I wouldn't stoop to it. You're the Mayor, for Christ's sake. Respect the office. Let them come to you.

Finnuala turns, direct.

Finnuala You keep saying how much you hate lunch, but if you remember, it was a lunch which got us where we are.

Moses I don't know what you're talking about.

Finnuala You know perfectly well. Sending Al Smith to eat with the judge.

Moses Where was that?

Finnuala You know where it was. At Riverhead.

Moses That was thirty years ago.

Finnuala Sure.

Moses It was no big deal.

Finnuala If we hadn't done it, we'd be nowhere. It all started there. Everything.

Moses In your opinion. That's just your opinion.

Moses has raised his voice at Finnuala, whose silence is eloquent. To divert, he looks angrily at Heller.

And there's a reason, is there, you're standing there like a lemon?

Heller Yes.

Moses So what is it?

Heller Washington Square.

Moses What about it?

Heller I was asked to take care of it.

Moses throws a look at Finnuala.

Finnuala You delegated, Bob. It's Mariah's patch.

She puts down the water, the pills and the liquid.

Moses What do I need to know?

Heller Well, sir, there's quite a strong residents' group forming –

Moses That I don't know already?

Heller A group who live in the Village, they're getting together –

Moses Women, are they?

Heller Mostly.

Moses Thought so.

Heller This group is well-educated, they're literate, they're extremely well-informed –

Moses I'm meant to be impressed?

Heller And if you remember, we promised them a public meeting.

Moses says nothing.

A meeting for them to put their objections. They want to keep the park a park.

Moses It will be a park.

Heller They don't think so. They think a road's going to change the whole feeling of the square. It'll be different.

Moses Of course it'll be different.

Heller It's going to be dissected by a sunken expressway.

Moses Exactly. Have they missed the word 'sunken'?

Heller No.

Moses And over the sunken expressway, I will place a pedestrian bridge, so that nursing mothers may push their baby carriages, and veterans may roll their wheelchairs. Life will go on as before.

He smiles, content.

I have promised: the two parts of Washington Square Park will be satisfactorily joined.

Heller They don't see it that way.

Moses That's because they're troublemakers. And they can't read a technical drawing. Who can?

Heller They're also worried about noise.

Moses If they're worried about noise, they shouldn't live in the city.

Heller They want a public meeting.

Moses I know what they want.

Heller I've asked you a few times. I don't think we can put them off any longer. I need you to give me a date.

Moses smiles.

Moses Tomorrow.

Heller Say what?

Moses At ten in the morning. They want a meeting, give them one. Hire a hall.

Heller A hall?

Moses We can't hold it in the street. Mr Porter'll go with you. The two of you can have breakfast. Anything you want. Scrambled eggs. Bacon. Have hash browns, I don't care. On expenses.

Heller And will you be coming?

Moses In person?

Heller Yes.

Moses I think not. I'm delegating, remember?

Moses is amused by the word.

Heller But, sir, are we really going to call a meeting that soon?

Moses Why not?

Heller Tomorrow morning?

Moses What's wrong with tomorrow?

Heller How to notify the interested parties.

Moses Oh.

Heller How they make themselves free. At such short notice.

Moses Call the organisers. They must have a figurehead.

Heller There's a woman.

Moses What sort of woman?

Heller She's an actress.

Moses Have I heard of her?

Heller Her name's Shirley Hayes.

Moses Then I'm sure she has time on her hands.

Heller And there's a journalist helping her –

Moses Then call them up. Put up some posters.

Heller Isn't that rather – well, aren't we –

Moses looks at her, irritable.

Moses What is your problem exactly, Miss Heller?

Heller I'm just saying –

Moses You seem to have a struggle with the English language.

Heller is taken aback by his rudeness. Moses swigs at the bottle of Pepto-Bismol.

You just said, these people are well-informed, well-educated.

Heller They live in the Village.

Moses With all their degrees and qualifications, surely they can read posters, can't they?

Heller But we have to give them fair notice, don't we?

Moses Legally?

Heller Yes.

Moses As it happens, not. It's our right to hold the meeting whenever we want. And they can all bring their guitars, and their poetry books, and all the other clutter of their well-stocked minds. I'm sure they can make themselves free. It's not as if these people have regular jobs.

He's amused. Heller isn't.

Heller I'm sorry, but it seems underhand. The protestors have wanted a meeting for months, and suddenly we throw one together so fast as to wrongfoot them.

Moses So where's the dishonesty? You keep reporting to me that they've been complaining about the endless delays.

Heller They have.

Moses So now they can't complain any more, can they?

He laughs.

Am I right, Finnuala?

Finnuala just looks at him.

Any objective observer would say we're tackling the matter with commendable dispatch.

Heller I really don't think it's right.

Moses You going to tell me why?

Heller For a start, I've read about your early days, Mr Moses. Opening up Long Island. You were an activist. Activism made you. And now these people are also activists. Also in a cause they believe in. Now it's their turn. And they deserve our respect.

Moses has been enjoying his own cleverness, but his mood changes.

Moses Mariah – it is, isn't it?

Heller It's Mariah –

Moses Mariah, I've given you a simple instruction. To organise a meeting for tomorrow.

Heller I know.

Moses So please go and do it.

Heller I'm not at peace.

Moses Then I'm going to have to ask you a question.

Heller waits, silent.

Whose side are you on, Mariah? That's my question. Whose side are you on?

Heller Forgive me for saying this, but your way of thinking is extremely old-fashioned.

Moses You think so, do you?

Heller The planner sits in the office and imposes his will. Nowadays people don't want to be told how to live, they want to choose how to live. And they have that right.

Moses is shaking his head.

Moses You know as well as I do that the traffic flows freely on Fifth Avenue until it reaches Eighth Street.

Heller Yes.

Moses Below Eighth Street, it's hopelessly congested. Am I right?

Heller It can be congested, yes. On occasions.

Moses I plan to serve the population – yes, *serve it* – by liberating that traffic with a well-planned highway which will funnel drivers straight through Washington Square and onwards into Lower Manhattan.

Heller I know the intention.

Heller swallows her emotions, and keeps calm.

All I can say, I've noticed in the months since I started, you seem to thrive on conflict and on confrontation.

Moses Do I?

Heller We were taught at school: the issue is never about winning or losing. It's about what's best for the community. And if, with the help of the community's input, we can improve our scheme, well, in my opinion, that's a good thing worth doing.

Moses nods, not rising to her, keeping his anger down.

Moses Very well, Mariah. You've given me your opinion. And I value it. Now, if you would, please find Mr Porter and call the meeting for tomorrow morning.

Heller I'll do what you want.

Moses That's kind of you.

Heller I've registered my objection.

Moses It's noted.

There is a silence. Heller picks up her stuff.

Heller Thank you for hearing me.

Moses Not at all.

Finnuala Well done, Mariah.

Finnuala smiles at her. Angry, Heller goes out. There's a silence. Then:

Moses Get rid of her.

Finnuala Sorry?

Moses She's not with us.

Finnuala Oh, Bob, come on –

Moses Let her call the meeting tomorrow, and then she goes.

Finnuala No.

Moses Finnuala, she's in the wrong job. She'll never be any good.

Finnuala Mariah's exactly what we need on Randall's Island. She puts us back in touch.

Moses You think I'm out of touch?

Finnuala No, but she's younger. She's closer to the ground.

He gets up, letting out his anger.

Moses Twenty years!

Finnuala I know –

Moses It's been twenty years!

Finnuala I know that –

Moses For twenty years I've planned a highway which would take traffic downtown –

Finnuala I remember –

Moses And onwards, remember! And onwards!

He stops, for assent. Finnuala is uncomfortable.

Finnuala Yes.

Moses And now finally the prize is in our grasp. What, I'm to throw the plan of a whole lifetime aside in favour of a group of minstrels and artistic women with handbags?

Finnuala looks at him reproachfully, not answering.

Outside the city, Finnuala, we've thrived. We've transformed the landscape. On Long Island. Upstate. Downstate. A network of roads and bridges. Unparalleled. The Romans built roads which have lasted two thousand years. Who's to say ours won't last as long?

He moves across the room, gathering energy.

And even inside the city itself – countless slums destroyed, tenements gone, to be replaced by efficient, clean housing blocks, pleasing to the eye and hygienic for the purpose of living. Clearance! Urban renewal! But in one aspect, and

93

one aspect of our work, we have failed. We have failed to give the borough of Manhattan the road system it deserves.

He points towards Long Island.

It's as if they want us out there, and to stay out there. Outsiders for ever. And never inside the citadel itself. We break Manhattan or it breaks us.

Finnuala just smiles.

Finnuala Bob, you exaggerate.

Moses I don't think so.

Finnuala You take everything too hard.

Moses And if I didn't, what would New York be? Just one more provincial city. A static port on the Eastern seaboard, between a couple of rivers, unbridged.

Finnuala looks at him, direct.

Finnuala You take it personally. It isn't personal.

Moses It's personal.

Finnuala No. It's the mood of the times.

Moses Oh, *that* excuse.

Finnuala It's not an excuse.

Moses A leader makes the mood, he's not a victim of it. I provide contracts. I provide jobs.

Finnuala is impatient.

Finnuala But things aren't that simple any more.

Moses Why not?

Finnuala People want to have a stake. They want to have a say.

Moses And they think they're qualified, do they?

Finnuala As qualified as anyone.

Moses Oh, really?

Finnuala Yes.

Moses Qualified to manage a huge metropolitan arterial complex, are they?

Finnuala Not as you are, no.

Moses No. As you say. Who provides the vision? Who provides the overview?

Moses smiles, having trapped her.

Once Americans cease to believe they can remake America better, then it ceases to be America.

Moses sits at his desk. He picks up a couple of files, and throws them haphazardly across the desk in a fit of bad temper.

And the worst thing is to see the change in you.

Finnuala What change?

Moses You know what I'm saying.

Finnuala On this occasion, no.

Moses Oh yes, you do.

Moses looks away, miserable.

How you once believed, and now you don't.

Finnuala I still believe.

Moses Then tell me, why are we not firing that girl?

Finnuala shrugs.

Finnuala You can fire her.

Moses What, and live with your disapproval?

95

Finnuala I can move to another office.

Moses I don't want that. I like you in here.

He sneaks a look at her, but she doesn't react.

Time was, you'd have got rid of her before I even asked.

Finnuala Time was.

Moses You brought her in. I was always against her. You can tell, she gets on my nerves.

Finnuala Everything gets on your nerves.

There is a silence.

Moses You would once have fired her. And now you won't. Why is that?

Finnuala You know very well the reason. She reminds me of me.

There is another silence, both of them thoughtful.

Moses When you were starting out?

Finnuala Exactly.

Moses When you were a girl?

Finnuala She has more money than I did –

Moses And less humour –

Finnuala She has a better background, her father's a professor –

Moses I might have known –

Finnuala Misfortune has not yet marked her.

Moses She's young.

Finnuala But she's in it not for herself but for the people.

Moses And you think I'm not?

Finnuala is silent a moment.

Finnuala Why trample on a flower when you don't need to?

Moses Is that what she is? Is that what you were?

There's a silence. Moses speaks very quietly.

Tell me something, Finnuala, would you ever resign from my employment?

Finnuala Me?

Moses Yes. Would I ever drive you to that?

There is a silence. Moses looks, then nods to himself.

Tell them to fix the meeting for the morning.

Finnuala I will.

THIRTEEN

At once the sound of Hayes' voice is heard among other angry shouts at what sounds like a well-attended meeting.

Hayes We saw what happened, we saw what happened in the Bronx. A great brutal carving knife slashed through the heart of a community – a community of the poorest and most powerless people in New York. Shipped out of town to God knows where. All for a road which was at a standstill on the very first day. If Mr Moses thinks he can pull the same trick twice, he's got another think coming.

Cheers. The public meeting assembles. With the activists, Hayes, Jacobs, McQuade, Mason, Amis and Savage are Heller and Porter, in a wheelchair. His grey hair is cropped, his legs powerless, early fifties, still courteous.

Is there no end to his vandalism? Where will it stop? Do you know what this place is?

Porter I think I do.

Hayes Do you know what it means? Not just to the people who live here? Do you know its historic importance?

Porter I certainly hope so.

Hayes This is New York's quintessential meeting place. And your boss intends to destroy it. With a four-lane highway. If Washington Square isn't safe, then where is?

There is applause and cheering.

Porter Excuse me, you asked for this meeting, and after twenty minutes, we've barely got a word out. What do you want? Anarchy?

Amis No. Democracy.

Everyone laughs.

Hayes This is our third year. This is our third consecutive year of opposition. I don't think you've ever understood the anger –

Porter I understand the anger very well.

Hayes Do you?

Porter Yes, indeed. I could hardly miss it. Miss Heller and I wouldn't be here if we didn't want to listen.

The protestors are quieted. Porter points to Jacobs.

Mrs Jacobs, you have a question?

Jacobs Perhaps you can tell us why Mr Moses isn't here in person –

Porter I don't know why you want to personalise this.

Jacobs Because it is personal.

Porter The highway is the policy of the whole Planning Commission.

Jacobs Mr Moses *is* the Planning Commission, we all know that. Why does he never meet his critics?

Porter He meets his critics all the time.

McQuade He's up in an ivory tower. He won't even interview. Lewis has tried. I've tried. He refuses to talk to us.

Mason He only speaks to people who agree with him.

Savage Oh yeah, he'll talk to the *New York Times*. Twice during the week and three times on Sundays.

Everyone laughs.

Jacobs It's Moses' ideas which are being copied all over the country. In every city in America, it's roads, roads, roads.

Porter If he's influential, it's for good reason.

Jacobs Then tell me this: why is Mr Moses so hostile to rapid transit?

Porter Is he hostile?

Jacobs Explain to me why he's built hundreds of miles of road, and not a single subway and not a single rail track? Not a single one – in twenty-five years!

There are murmurs of approval. Porter looks to Heller.

Porter Do you want to take this, Mariah?

Heller No, you take it.

Porter Very well. Are you sure?

Heller I'd rather you.

Porter smiles reassuringly at her.

Porter Just tell me, Mrs Jacobs, I'm happy to debate with you, but, honestly, what does Mr Moses' attitude to mass transit have to do with Washington Square?

Jacobs Everything, I'd have thought.

Porter Why?

Jacobs Because Mr Moses is a man under hypnosis.

Laughter.

He got hypnotised at the age of twenty-five by two ideas and they're both delusions.

Porter And what are they?

Jacobs First, he has this insane idea that the answer to the problem of too many cars is more cars. And second, he's convinced the answer to the problem of congestion on our roads is more roads.

Porter Mrs Jacobs, you and your friends can hardly deny New York has a problem with congestion.

Jacobs And what will you do by building a new road, except move the whole problem further south? It won't go away. The jams will just happen further downtown. Haven't you people learned anything from the last thirty years?

It's out of hand again. Porter raises his arm to quiet the crowd. No effect. Heller gets upset and stands up.

Heller Please, everyone, please. You have to listen to Mr Porter, you really do.

Savage Why?

Heller I'll tell you why. I only joined the Planning Commission eight months ago, but I realised on the day I arrived that Ariel really is a man who is utterly sincere and dedicated in making the city as liveable as he can. Please.

Such an honest young woman standing up stills the objectors.

Porter Thank you, Mariah, that's kind of you. Thank you. Mrs Jacobs?

Jacobs starts again in a much more conciliatory tone.

Jacobs Every time Mr Moses builds a new road, he says it's going to free up the highways and make car journeys shorter, and get us all home to look after our children and be saintly to our wives. And you know what happens in reality?

Porter Please. Go ahead. I'd love to know.

Jacobs Cars in New York, Mr Porter, move slower than the horses they replaced. And to make his precious roads, Mr Moses smashes ahead by violence. That's what he's done in the Bronx with his disastrous expressway.

But Porter is on to her.

Porter Oh, you think the tenements we knocked down in the Bronx were worthwhile, do you, Mrs Jacobs? You think slums are worthwhile?

Mason She's not saying that.

Porter You want to preserve them, do you?

Mason That's not what she's saying.

Amis People lived in those slums.

Porter You're right. They lived in those uninhabitable places, full of rats and dark and dirt. And you want to preserve them because you don't have to live in them. It's very easy for you, Mrs Jacobs, to wave a privileged hand and say 'Oh these slums are so picturesque.'

Savage If you think Jane's privileged, you know nothing about her.

There are some smiles, but Porter has the bit between his teeth.

Porter Truly, there's an element of snobbery in all this. A city has to change if it's to live. I can see you all want to set up an opposition. Planners bad, people good. But it isn't as simple as that. In Washington Square, you have something special, people can stroll, they can play chess, they can make music, and sure, if I lived here, among other educated folk, I'd want to defend it too. But doesn't it concern you that the city will die if the lucky few just hang on to their favourite corners, and don't make any arrangements to help people elsewhere?

Jacobs Oh, so we all have to live at a common level of ugliness?

Porter No.

McQuade That's what he's saying. Everything has to be dragged down to the level of the worst.

Porter No, I'm not saying that. I'm saying a good road will help people less fortunate than you speed down to their own quarter. And unimpeded movement is in everyone's interest. Can't you be more generous to others? Can't you think about the good of other people, not just the people in the nice parts of town?

There is silence at this rebuke.

I've worked for Mr Moses for over thirty years. Mr Moses never claimed the car would solve mankind's problems, any more than the refrigerator or the dishwasher would. But whether you like it or not, the car is the future. We have no future unless we work with the grain of progress, not against it.

FOURTEEN

Heller steps out of the action, with an air of amusement and addresses us.

Heller There was a funny tone to that meeting. I noticed it straight away. For a start, mothers had brought their kids. It wasn't just people saying no. It was people who actually had different ideas.

We'd never heard of Jane Jacobs. Who had? She looked like a housewife. That's why no one had noticed her.

Robert Moses had driven an expressway right through the South Bronx. And he'd opened up Long Island.

So he had history. He'd beaten the slum-dwellers and he'd beaten the aristocrats. But now he'd taken on a far deadlier enemy – the one no one ever beats.

This time he was fighting the middle classes.

FIFTEEN

Randall's Island office. As before, but this time late at night. Heller moves back to join Porter who is already at a table working. The two of them work at papers for a while till Moses comes in, grim, in an overcoat. He hangs it behind the door.

Moses You waited for me.

Porter Yes.

Moses goes to sit at his desk. Porter seems nervous.

How was it?

Moses As bad as you'd expect.

Porter I'm sorry.

Moses I don't want to talk about it.

Porter I didn't mean to intrude.

Heller has not moved a muscle.

Moses And you, Miss Heller? You stayed also?

Heller Yes.

Moses I'm wondering, do you have a young man?

Heller I do. As a matter of fact.

Moses He waits for you in the evening?

Heller He's studying to be a doctor. So he works late as well.

Moses But who works later?

Heller Almost always me.

Moses Good.

He nods, with grim satisfaction. Porter looks nervously towards Heller.

Porter We have bad news.

Moses Is that the only reason you stayed?

Porter No, no, I stayed to be sure you were all right.

Moses I'm all right. Why would I not be?

Porter I was concerned for you.

Moses Park your concern.

Porter And also, to bring you up to date.

Porter hesitates a moment.

Eleanor Roosevelt has joined the committee.

Moses Mrs Roosevelt?

Porter Yes.

Moses And which committee has she joined?

Porter To save Washington Square.

Moses shrugs.

Moses Isn't that what we'd expect?

Porter Maybe.

Moses Is there a vexatious cause in America which does not attract her support? As long as Mrs Roosevelt can display herself as virtuous thereby.

Porter Yes.

Moses Well then.

Porter But she's also written a column.

Moses Where?

Porter In the *New York Post*. It appears tomorrow.

Moses You have a copy?

Porter nods and holds it up.

Porter Do you want to read it?

Moses Hardly. Goethe, yes. Schiller, yes. Aristotle, regularly. But the Roosevelts, no. Never in my life.

Moses shrugs.

What does she tell us? Give me the gist.

Porter She says the highway will destroy the essential character of the neighbourhood. It should be postponed.

Moses nods, serious.

Moses And the more important question?

Porter Yes?

Moses Has Mrs Roosevelt spotted where it's going?

Porter No. Nobody has.

Moses I never see that woman without wanting to punch her stupid liberal face.

Moses returns to work.

Porter And is that it?

Moses Sorry?

Porter You feel we can just leave it at that?

Moses What would you prefer me to do?

Porter I'm asking if you want to reply.

Moses To the *New York Post*?

Porter Yes.

Moses To a woman with a grievance?

Porter I'm not sure what her grievance is.

Moses The world is leaving her behind. Her husband was unfaithful. Nobody likes her. Take your pick.

Moses continues working.

Porter She points out the paradox.

Moses What paradox is that?

Porter She says you made your name creating parks. Now you want to destroy one.

Moses Sure. Tell her from me, I'll still be ahead, won't I?

Moses grins.

I've doubled the green space in New York City to thirty-five thousand acres. I've added zoos, recreation centres, ball fields, seventeen miles of beach and six hundred and fifty-eight playgrounds. Tell her my conscience is at peace and to go fuck herself.

Porter I'd like to but I can't.

Moses Why not?

Porter Because she says something else.

Moses What else?

Heller She suggests closing the square to traffic altogether.

Moses sits back.

Moses That's her plan, is it?

Heller Yes.

Moses That's her idea?

Heller Yes.

Moses It's doomed. It's ridiculous.

Porter I fear it may capture the public imagination. She believes cars are strangling the city, and that certain areas should be closed to them.

Moses Does she indeed?

Porter She says all Mr Moses wants is for cars to flow. What she wants is for people to get out of their cars and walk.

Moses Is she out of her head?

Moses gets up.

I'm almost inclined to let her have her way. Does she have any idea what will happen on Eighth Street?

Porter She deals with that point.

Moses Can she imagine the level of congestion?

Porter She believes, on the contrary, that once people are told to avoid a particular route, they will take care not to find themselves anywhere near a potential trouble spot.

Moses She believes that, does she?

Porter Far from increasing the traffic in the areas around the square, she believes closing the square will actually have the effect of thinning it.

Porter shrugs.

I'm just reporting.

Moses And what is her suggested evidence for this theory?

Porter She has none. She simply believes that people will behave sensibly. Once warned of a closure, they will avoid it.

Moses turns, nodding.

Moses Just remind me, will you, Ariel, of Mrs Roosevelt's age?

Porter Her age?

Moses Yes. How old is she?

Heller I happen to know this.

Porter Do you?

Heller We were taught at school. Eleanor Roosevelt was born in 1884.

Porter 1884? That makes her – let's think –

But Moses is ahead of him, already pacing.

Moses So, I have learned something. There exists on earth a human being who has achieved three score years and ten, and who still believes in the natural good sense and intelligence of the common people.

He turns, laughing.

'Once warned of a closure, they will avoid it'! Does she have any idea?

Porter I fear not.

Moses I don't know whether to envy Mrs Roosevelt her gullibility or to despise her for it.

He shakes his head, and heads back to work.

Let's press ahead.

Porter We can't. As of this moment.

Moses We're still waiting?

Porter Yes. For the Mayor to sign off on the whole scheme.

Moses Doesn't he realise? Doesn't he know?

Porter He knows.

Moses How important it is. We have developers – private developers – building hundreds of apartments. Developing Washington Square Village. These are business people.

People from the world of commerce. I promised them access. I promised them a road. I gave them my word.

He stands, furious. But Porter is long past being scared of him.

Porter Then you'll just have to break it, won't you?

Finnuala is standing at the door. She is in a coat, as if she's blown in like a ghost. Moses stares at her.

Moses And what are you doing here? You went home.

Finnuala I came back.

Moses Why?

Finnuala Ariel called me. You've been to the asylum.

Moses Yes.

Finnuala I guessed you'd come on here.

Moses You were right.

Finnuala Does she know where she is?

Moses shakes his head.

Has she been sedated?

Moses Yes.

Finnuala How was she?

Moses looks, ice-cold. Finnuala repeats the question.

How was she?

Moses And we say psychiatric clinic, but it's the same thing.

Finnuala What have you been doing?

Moses Continuing to work. What else should I do?

Finnuala Is there anything I can get you?

Moses No. And in the circumstances, thank you, a drink least of all.

He goes back to his desk.

It seems I'm suddenly an object of sympathy, and that's not a role I relish. You should all go to bed.

He sits down at the desk and pulls a huge number of files towards him. Finnuala looks to Heller and Porter. Heller shifts.

Heller Well, as it happens, it's getting on for when I said I'd see David –

Moses You're meeting your medical friend tonight?

Heller Yes.

Moses Where?

Heller In a bar. Downtown. Greenwich Village.

Heller looks down at the coincidence.

It's cosy there.

Moses How nice. It's a nice area. Have a drink with your nice young man. And be grateful your life is just starting.

Finnuala Have a good evening, Mariah.

Heller I will. And may I say something before I go?

Moses Please do.

Heller You're no different from anyone else, Mr Moses. Sometimes you're right and sometimes you're wrong.

Moses Thank you, Miss Heller.

Heller I sat through that meeting about Washington Square and I can tell you right now you're beaten. There's a new feeling in the air, and it's going to change things. You've lost the argument. And when you refuse to admit it, you make us all look undignified. Goodnight.

Heller goes out. Moses doesn't react, lost in his thoughts.

Finnuala It's Payne Whitney?

Moses Sorry?

Finnuala Mary's at Payne Whitney?

Moses Oh. Yes.

Finnuala It's not a weakness, Bob, to talk about your wife!

Moses In front of strangers?

Finnuala Oh, we're strangers, are we? You, me and Ariel, what, a hundred years of work together between the three of us?

Moses I meant the coloured girl.

Finnuala She's gone.

Moses That didn't stop you.

Moses looks away.

Mary's an alcoholic. What can I say? She's lost control. The drink has gone to her brain. It's eaten her away.

Finnuala How long will she stay?

Moses The doctors, right at this moment, don't believe she will leave.

Moses shrugs.

You know how we were together.

Finnuala Yes.

Moses She paid my bills, she bought my clothes. Hell, she cut my hair. There's nothing in my life she didn't do for me.

There is a silence.

There it is.

Finnuala Oh Bob –

Moses A lifetime.

He drums his fingers a moment on the table.

There is nothing to be done, except to absorb the blow and continue to build. I owe it to her.

Moses puts his jaw out, defying them to reply.

Porter Perhaps, if you'd like us to cover for you . . .

Moses Cover?

Porter Yes.

Porter Just for a few days. So you can be with Mary.

Moses That won't be necessary.

Porter I was just suggesting.

Moses turns, changing the subject.

Moses So, Finnuala, have you heard our news?

Finnuala What news?

Moses Ariel has it. About Mrs Roosevelt. And her journalism.

Porter holds up a copy of the Post.

Finnuala Yes, I heard.

Moses What do you think?

Finnuala says nothing.

I'm asking, what do you think?

Finnuala Truthfully?

Moses How else?

Finnuala It's only the beginning. The tide is turning. It's turning slowly, but it's turning. Worse is to come.

Moses You know something I don't?

Moses sits back, staring at her.

Why do you say 'beginning'?

Finnuala As I came here, I promised myself I'd spare you.

Moses Why?

Finnuala Because your wife is lying drugged in an institution after forty years of marriage! That's why!

Moses I thought you were about to say after forty years of neglect.

Finnuala I was not!

Moses All right!

Moses has shouted back. Finnuala has turned red, her temper high.

You think I don't feel your rebuke?

Finnuala What rebuke?

Moses The silent rebuke. Daily. Unspoken. I sit in this room with you. I feel it.

Finnuala No.

Moses You blame me.

Finnuala No.

Moses You think her illness is my fault.

Finnuala I have never said that.

Moses Implicitly.

Finnuala No.

Moses Because I work and work and care for nothing else.

He turns suddenly to Porter, furious.

Cover for me, would you?

Finnuala tries to control her own anger.

You think I don't know what you say about me, behind my back, one to another?

Finnuala Please. If you feel guilty, that's your business.

Moses You think I'm a brute. I'm not.

Finnuala Don't blame your own misgivings on Ariel. Or on me.

Moses I have no guilt.

Finnuala Good.

Moses And I have no remorse. I can't be bullied into feelings I don't have.

Finnuala I would never try.

Moses Apologies are for cowards only.

Finnuala How you've lived your life is your own affair. As is mine. As is Ariel's, too.

Porter waves a protesting hand.

Porter Leave me out of it.

Finnuala All these years, you've watched Ariel suffer. You've worked with him, side by side. You've watched him fall prey to a terrible disease –

Porter Finnuala –

Finnuala Well, that's what's happened! Without once, as I remember, ever once so much as remarking on it! Not in my hearing! Ever!

Porter I have not asked to be remarked upon.

Finnuala That's nothing to do with it.

Porter When the moment arrives when I can no longer function, I shall leave.

Moses is glowering from behind the desk.

Finnuala It's multiple sclerosis, Bob.

Moses I know.

Finnuala That's what Ariel deals with every day.

Moses I know that perfectly well.

Finnuala Every hour!

Moses Do you think I don't know that?

Finnuala First day when he came through on crutches, what did you ask? Nothing. You didn't mention it. Later in a wheelchair. Again, all you ask 'Oh God, will we have to widen the door?'

Moses I did not say that!

Finnuala That's what you said. I remember it as it if were yesterday!

They are shouting. Porter is hating this.

Porter I don't ask for pity.

Finnuala I'm not talking about pity. I'm talking about consideration. And that Mr Moses has never given you.

Porter I've never complained.

Moses See? He's fine.

Finnuala Oh, I know. We're all professional colleagues, no more than that. God forbid we should think each other friends.

Moses I have never asked for friendship.

Finnuala Indeed, you have not.

Moses I have preferred respect.

Finnuala And that you had.

Moses Had?

Finnuala Yes.

Moses *Had?*

Finnuala I'm saying, let's leave this whole sorry business for tonight. For Mary's sake.

Moses No!

Moses has roared, all his anger and frustration in a single word.

If you have something to tell me, tell me. I can take it.

Finnuala hesitates.

Finnuala If you really want to know, the Mayor has been indiscreet.

Moses Tell me.

Finnuala Accidentally.

Moses How?

Finnuala He has spoken to Shirley Hayes.

Moses The actress?

Finnuala Yes. Unintentionally.

Moses She leads the protest?

Finnuala Yes.

Moses Why did they meet?

Finnuala She asked to see him.

Moses And why did he agree?

Finnuala The Mayor is elected. Unlike us, he has to listen.

Moses is sullen, grumpy.

Moses So tell me, what did he say?

Finnuala Too much.

Moses Specifically?

There is a brief silence.

Finnuala I fear he revealed the real purpose of the highway through Washington Square.

Moses shakes his head.

Moses I can't believe it!

Finnuala I'm afraid so.

Moses How could he do that? What foolishness made him do that? God, am I surrounded by idiots?

Finnuala You might as well face it: you can't keep everything under wraps for ever.

Moses Oh, can't I?

Finnuala It was bound to come out. People aren't stupid. They know your ambition. They know your track record. And now they have proof.

Moses has got up, disbelieving.

Moses It's simple. It's perfectly simple. We are addressing a logical discrepancy, which it's my civic duty to set right. Look at the map!

Finnuala I've looked.

Moses Look at the network!

Finnuala I've seen it. Many times.

Moses The vertical observed. The horizontal ignored. Look!

He goes to the big map on the wall, where all his roads are marked. Porter looks to Finnuala in despair.

Look!

Porter We don't need to look. How many times have we stared at that map?

Moses What kind of city have we created where the roads run up and down, but nothing runs across?

Porter We've discussed this. We've discussed it many times.

Moses Our work is not finished. It's barely half-done.

Porter We know.

He runs his hand down the map, dynamically.

Moses North to South, on either side, the West Side Highway, the East Side Highway, traffic carried efficiently and with speed to its destination.

Porter Sure.

Moses And across the city? Nothing! East to West? Nothing! It's an offence against logic. And against reason.

He sweeps his arm across the map.

The need is there, clearly, for three elevated expressways – here, here and here – like staples – like hoops of steel – so that sideways movement across the city becomes possible. The expressways and parkways of Long Island will connect directly to the expressways and parkways of New Jersey. At last New York State is opened up – one piece, one entity. And the city itself becomes an authentic grid. What could be more desirable than that? Manhattan will shrink to become a mere island which it is possible to cross and put behind you. From one borough to another. Manhattan will no longer be the sinking sand in which lateral traffic spins its wheels aimlessly in mud.

Moses turns to them.

Please tell me, who would not be happy with that?

Finnuala shrugs.

Finnuala Since you ask, it seems quite a lot of people –

Moses Like who?

Finnuala Like the people who live in Manhattan for a start.

Moses All of them, Finnuala?

Finnuala No.

Moses Is everyone against me?

Finnuala No. I can't say that.

Finnuala shakes her head.

But tell me, if it's all so logical and desirable, as you claim, why did we not publish the scheme in the first place?

Moses I'm not ashamed of it, if that's what you're implying.

Finnuala Aren't you?

Moses No.

Finnuala Then why did you forbid us to speak of it? Why is it such a great secret that no one outside this room even knows of it?

Moses is restless, discontent.

Moses It will be published.

Finnuala You promise?

Moses I don't need to promise.

Finnuala When?

Moses At my own speed.

Finnuala Why not now? Why not tonight? Why not respond to this misfortune by coming clean?

Moses turns, furious.

Moses Because, as you know, people characteristically revolt against any innovation.

Finnuala Is that right?

Moses When advancing any plan, experience teaches us to be strategic.

Finnuala Is that the word?

Moses What word would you prefer?

Finnuala For the way we behave? The word I would use is 'dishonest'.

Moses looks at her, not answering.

What other word am I to use? In the circumstances? Ask Ariel.

Porter I'm staying out of this.

Finnuala All right.

Porter has again put up his hands in self-defence.

You put Ariel out there to defend a scheme to the community when he's not allowed to reveal what the real purpose of that scheme is.

Moses There was no need to reveal it.

Finnuala You sent Mariah with him. She's a girl, her head full of Mies van der Rohe and Frank Lloyd Wright. You forced her to lie.

Moses I did no such thing.

Finnuala In public. At her first public hearing. Ariel?

Porter shrugs slightly.

Porter We were both compromised, yes, it's true.

Finnuala Thank you.

Porter Obviously, we were in a difficult position. We described the highway as clearly as we could, but we could not reveal the reason for it. We were walking on eggshells.

Moses shrugs.

Finnuala You sent them out there to talk about relieving congestion. As though that were the purpose of the road.

Moses In part, it is.

Finnuala No. The purpose of the road is to carry downtown traffic towards a new cross-town expressway. That is the sole reason for its existing.

Moses It's the principal reason, yes.

Finnuala Another way of putting it: you intend to turn Washington Square into an on-ramp.

Moses Something has to be done!

He bangs the table.

Is there anyone else who will dare to take this city's problems in hand? Who else can do it? For every dozen men with bright ideas there is at most one who can execute them.

Finnuala gets up and points to the map.

Finnuala You intend to send an expressway along between Broome Street and Grand.

Moses Correct.

Finnuala Knocking down some of the greatest industrial architecture in America.

Moses Oh please! Do you really fall for that stuff?

Finnuala What stuff?

Moses Conservation.

Finnuala Fall for it?

Moses It's a racket.

Finnuala In your view.

Moses Run by women. To put a brake on progress. What's its purpose? What's its point?

Finnuala What's its point?

Moses Yes.

Finnuala To hold on to everything that is best.

Moses No. It's a plot. It's a conspiracy. Dreamt up by liberals to make sure the United States is embalmed in aspic for ever.

Finnuala Oh really!

Moses You doubt me? Here it is, the most developed country in the world, with limitless resources and, all at once, fashionable opinion tells us that we can't build. We can't bring prosperity to those who need it, because those who already enjoy it don't like the noise! They have a pleasant life for themselves and they wish to deny it to others.

Finnuala It's not about that.

Moses Isn't it?

Finnuala No.

Moses Ask me what I see in SoHo and I see one thing. Decline. Yes, we may have to destroy a few useless lofts and abandoned premises. So what?

He points a finger at Finnuala, spelling out his mantra.

Things must exist for a purpose. SoHo has no purpose. Vitality is dependent on function. And when function decays, so does life.

Finnuala looks him in the eye, putting a question she has longed to ask.

Finnuala And do you really never look at anything – anything at all – and consider it might be beautiful in itself?

Moses The principal purpose of planning is to improve peoples' lives. SoHo improves nothing. It's one big fire hazard.

Finnuala smiles, sardonic.

Finnuala Well as of this evening, it no longer matters.

Moses Why not?

Finnuala Because everything is changed. Things are out in the open.

Moses I welcome the fight. I've fought all my life.

Finnuala Yes. With the wind behind you. Now the wind is in front.

Moses shakes his head.

You didn't hear Mariah, did you? You didn't listen. It's a shame because she was trying to tell you something. Shirley Hayes and people like her, they're new, they're different. You call them liberals, because they dress in raincoats and have untidy hair. But Washington Square isn't a movement, it's a coalition. Of all parties.

Moses says nothing.

And it's hard to admit it, Bob. It's hard for you and it's hard for me. Because we've staked so much on being right. When Mariah arrived, I disregarded her. Of course I did. She's just out of school. What does she know? Then slowly I realised what she knows. She knows what's going on. And I'll tell you what I hear when I hear her speak, so young, so fresh. It's the sound of my life going by.

Finnuala nods.

I've waited for you to change and you don't. You should go to the meetings. And if you refuse, it's as Mariah says. You'll lose.

Moses And you think I deserve to lose? Do you relish the prospect of my defeat? Does it give you pleasure?

There is a silence. Porter looks between them.

Porter I'm sorry, I have to go home.

Moses Yes, if you have to.

Porter My driver's outside and he doesn't like to be late back to his wife.

Moses Well, that's fair enough.

Porter He has a life.

Moses Then he's fortunate. Go, please.

Porter I'm going.

Porter turns his wheelchair to go. Awkwardly Moses gets up, wanting to speak.

Moses Ariel, I do hope you don't feel that I'm ever callous with your illness.

Porter No, you're not callous.

Moses Thank you.

Porter Not at all.

Moses Good.

Porter You never even notice it, so how can you be callous?

Porter smiles, as gentle and humorous as ever.

Moses Forgive me. Sometimes I'm aware, I can be a little bit distracted.

Porter Yes.

Moses My mind's not always on the other man.

Porter nods slightly.

Porter Lucky you've still got time to work on that, then.

He smiles at Finnuala.

Goodnight, Finnuala.

Finnuala Goodnight.

Porter Goodnight, sir.

Moses Goodnight.

Porter turns and goes. There is a silence. The room is further darkened, the two of them alone.

And suddenly it's bad between us.

Finnuala Yes. It's bad.

There's a short silence.

Moses I've always feared lassitude. I've feared inertia. Life has to go forwards.

Finnuala Once you believed in cars because you thought they would liberate people. Now you force people into cars and you force cars onto roads because you want to be vindicated. It's no longer about the people. It's about you.

Moses looks at her resentfully.

Moses People like cars. You own something and you're in control. That's a nice feeling. When I was young, America was sitting there, like a tin can. The car was the can opener. Still is.

Finnuala Then I'll ask something.

Moses Sure.

Finnuala Why have you never learned to drive yourself?

Moses smiles slightly.

So many miles of highway we've built, so many hundreds of miles, and in that whole time you've not driven one.

Moses I had no need to. I had someone to drive for me.

Finnuala Not even for pleasure, then?

Moses No.

Finnuala Not even for Mary?

Moses Mary, again.

He has spoken almost to himself.

Finnuala You see, I never worried at first why you were so against public transportation. When we built the bridges over the road to Jones Beach, remember, and we built them so low buses couldn't go under? What was the reason? You must have had a reason. You can tell me now. After all it was a long time ago.

Moses stares at her, not answering.

All right then, why didn't we build rapid transit? Why have we never built rapid transit? We could have built a train. In fact, Al Smith – you worshipped Al Smith – I specifically remember, the Governor ordered you to build a train.

Moses He did.

Finnuala Then why not?

Again, Moses doesn't answer.

And such a fuss we made about democracy! I seem to remember: we were building the democratic beach.

Moses So we did.

Finnuala Oh yes sure, we built a beach for the people. Two splendid bath-houses in Barbizon brick, in Egyptian relief, and a campanile to set them off. A theatre for fifteen thousand, like the Coliseum. The finest people's beach in the world. But only for the kind of people you like.

Moses I'm not sure what you mean by that.

Finnuala Clean people, Bob. Well-off people, Bob. White people.

Finnuala gets up and walks to the window.

And what we've been doing these last few years. Look at that!

Moses What about it?

Finnuala When we went through the Bronx. Knocking down buildings and destroying communities. Do we ever stop and think who's in those communities?

There is a silence.

Slum clearance, we call it. Tell you what slum clearance really means. Getting rid of the Negroes, that's what it means.

Moses It's just a fact. The poorest people live in the worst houses. Their colour makes no difference to me. We move people out. And so we should. We take them out of dirty places and we move them to cleaner places. We cut out the cancerous tissue. If you leave things as they are, they rot.

Finnuala shakes her head.

Finnuala There's a bias in everything this office does, and it's a bias towards the better off.

Moses Finnuala, you know full well: people may not like me, but they need me.

Finnuala They have needed you, yes.

Moses And now of course it's suddenly fashionable to dislike me, because I'm the dirty bastard who pushed through the things democracy needed, but which democracy couldn't deliver. Secretly, people know that.

And they know I'm necessary. And as long as I go on doing what they need, you can be sure I'll be taking the rap.

Finnuala You're stuck. You're stuck with an idea you had thirty years ago. And you can't move on. Is there anything worse than being trapped in a dream?

Finnuala looks at him a moment.

I'm leaving, Bob.

Moses Leaving?

Finnuala Yes.

Moses But you said –

Finnuala I know –

Moses Only a few weeks ago –

Finnuala Yes –

Moses When I asked you –

Finnuala Yes.

Moses Tell me, what have I done? What have I done wrong?

Finnuala shakes her head, amused.

Finnuala It isn't like that.

Moses I'll make it up to you.

Finnuala That's not what I'm saying.

Moses Whatever it is.

Finnuala It's not one thing.

Moses What is it then? Finnuala, you've given your life to this work.

Finnuala Yes. Exactly. I've given my life. Maybe that's it.

Moses frowns.

Moses I've learned a lot.

Finnuala Yes.

Moses In the thirty years. I've adapted.

Finnuala You've adapted. Yes. But you haven't changed.

Finnuala nods, certain now.

And I've lived half a life.

Moses Yes, I know that.

Finnuala I lost a child.

Moses I know.

Finnuala Liam was six months old. And my husband left me.

Moses You're not blaming me?

Finnuala No.

Moses waits, not understanding.

And now Mary is ill.

Moses Yes.

Finnuala As you say, beyond curing.

Moses I fear.

Finnuala Lost to you.

Finnuala looks at him.

Don't you think the moment comes when we need to put down our maps and our plans, and maybe look around us?

Moses stands a moment, staring.

Moses I'm going to lose you, Finnuala. I know when your mind's made up. That's going to be a hard blow. And I don't quite know why you want to deliver it on the day Mary goes into the hospital.

Finnuala But, don't you see, that's exactly why I want to deliver it.

Moses If this is the end of it, I tell you, I'd rather be right and alone, than be soft and with other people. I'd rather that. My God, I'd rather that.

Finnuala looks, knowing she can't reach him.

Oh, they'll call it the Robert Moses Expressway, or the Robert Moses Park. They'll say 'Robert Moses, the architect of modern New York.' While working all the time, naturally, to undermine me, to get rid of me, for no other reason but that I'm right.

He nods, affirmed.

I did what no one else could do. And it stands, providing a frame for the way New Yorkers live. Giving them a structure that's going to last. And all of you fall away as we do it. Yes, even you, Finnuala, not able to see things through. I alone. I alone see things through. And don't talk to me about life, because that's the life I chose. Yes, maybe fashion's going to blow my kind of thinking right away. But I'll tell you one thing about fashion. One day it'll blow right back in.

He nods, satisfied.

Now come in, please, one day and clear your desk when I'm not here. I don't want to see you leaving –

Finnuala Fine –

Moses Choose a time when I'm out on the job. God knows, such a moment won't be hard to find.

Finnuala You'll be as busy as ever.

Moses Busier. I'll be out on the George Washington Bridge, planning how to double-deck it.

Finnuala Sure.

Moses Or I'll be out to see where the Bergen County Expressway should be. And the Throgs Neck Expressway. And the Clearway Expressway. And the Cross-Bronx Expressway extension. And the Gowanus and the Clove Lakes. And building an arts complex at Lincoln Square, because who else can they ask?

He smiles, grim.

If you want to leave, it won't be hard to find a time.

Finnuala Good. I'll do it, Bob.

She gets up and goes to put her coat on. Moses sits down at his desk to work, as though nothing had happened.

I'll leave the stair lights on for you.

Moses Thank you.

Finnuala And you'd better have my key.

She puts it down on his desk. He doesn't look up.

Moses If you need a reference, I'm happy to give you one.

Finnuala That's kind of you.

Moses After all.

They look at each other.

We had good times.

Finnuala We certainly did.

Moses They were fine times.

He nods to himself.

Any idea what you might be going to?

Finnuala Honest to God, I hadn't got round to thinking. Maybe something which doesn't involve knocking things down.

Moses I can call a few people if you like. Call in a few favours. God knows, people owe me.

Finnuala I won't need that, thanks. I'd rather do it on my own.

She smiles and goes out. Moses works a few moments, writing at his desk, and only after a while does he look up. As he does so, Jacobs appears.

SIXTEEN

Jacobs A couple of years later, the city sealed Washington Square off from traffic altogether. Nobody complained. Then, by community action, we stopped the cross-town expressways, and SoHo survived. Survived and was reborn.

Porter appears in his wheelchair.

Porter When the 1960s came, Governor Rockefeller got rid of Moses. He'd enjoyed forty years of continuous power. I stayed with him to the end.

Jacobs Me, I moved my family to Toronto at the end of the sixties, because I wanted my sons to avoid the draft. I was done with the US by then.

Porter The World's Fair in 1965 was kind of a fiasco because Moses refused to build a subway extension to get people there. After all, a subway would have transported just anyone at all.

Porter smiles. Music, deep, romantic, begins to play. Finnuala appears and talks to us.

Finnuala 'Vitality is dependent on function, and when function decays, so does life.' Bob Moses never lived to see the day when the car became man's enemy, not his friend.

Jacobs I was lucky. I'd known New York when everyone, from all backgrounds, lived together. But our efforts to preserve Greenwich Village and SoHo succeeded in transforming it into the most expensive piece of real estate in the world. What was once a community was cleansed of everyone but the rich. The Village was saved, but it was also destroyed.

Whether that was Robert Moses' fault or whether it was mine, I really can't say.

Jacobs turns and goes. So does Porter. Finnuala is left alone.

Finnuala The city changed, but Bob couldn't. A dream's a wonderful thing, but you need to make sure you can climb out of it.

Moses appears. Music, deep, romantic. Finnuala and he are on opposite sides of the stage.

Moses Life's not so great for a lot of people. A drive in the country, a day at the beach and you may forget.

The beach, the sea, the sky appears behind them.

I walk the strand. I love it. I take off my clothes and I swim. I swim as far out as I dare. And then when I begin to get frightened, I swim out further.